WHAT
THE BIBLE
TEACHES
ABOUT
THE HOLY
SPIRIT

WHAT THE BIBLE TEACHES ABOUT

THE
HOLY
SPIRIT

John Peck

SERIES EDITOR: G. W. KIRBY

Tyndale House Publishers, Inc. Wheaton, Illinois

Unless otherwise stated, biblical quotations are from the *Revised Standard Version* of the Bible.

Library of Congress Catalog Card Number 79-64985. ISBN 0-8423-7882-0. Copyright © 1979 by John Peck. First published in Great Britain by Kingsway Publications, Ltd. Tyndale House edition published by arrangement with Kingsway Publications, Ltd. All rights reserved. First Tyndale House printing, July 1979. Printed in the United States of America.

CONTENTS

PREFACE

God undoubtedly intends us to know him, and it takes very little thought to realize that the only one who could proclaim him adequately would have to be God himself. So it is perfectly understandable that the one who reveals to us God the Father will be God the Son. But Christ is not present with us in the flesh now, so who can reveal him to us? Undoubtedly, God the Holy Spirit. But the fact is that to many Christians the phrase 'the Holy Spirit' is itself something of an enigma.

This book may seem to ignore many of the disputes among Christians about some aspects of doctrine, for instance on the sacraments, and questions like what happened to the 'old nature' at conversion, and so on. But what I have tried to do is to indicate and explain the *basic* ideas to be found in Scripture. On these ideas others may well be built up, and they may be important too. But such matters lie beyond the scope of this book. There is a list of books for those who want to study further.

Something needs to be said about the way the Bible is used. The chapters are headed with a number of Scripture readings. This is designed to help the reader to get the main weight of the Bible's own language, and it may help him to read the chapter without too much stopping to hunt out Bible references.

The need to get the overall impact of the Bible's words is important, for two reasons. One is that much of the doctrine has to be worked out, not from plain statements of information, but by a kind of detective work, deducing the facts of the matter from the way that, in some passages, the Spirit is said to act, or the way people speak of him. I do endeavour to give Bible references for what is to be taught, but sometimes the connection may need a little meditation and thought.

The second reason is that, very largely, the day of 'proof-texts' seems to be over. There is a great variety of modern translations giving a good deal of diversity in the rendering of single texts. One sympathizes with Punch's remark of a London bus driver at the advent of the new asphalt roads: 'We all has our improvements to put up with.' One result is that it has become very difficult to settle an argument among Christians simply by quoting a text. In a way, this is all to the good. The New Testament writers tended to use groups of texts in their teaching, and they aimed at using typically biblical language to express the main thrust of the Bible's message. The Bible for them was not so much a store of ammunition as a fortress or a man o' war. This is partly why I have not felt obliged to keep to only one translation, and often a paraphrase is given to bring out a particular line of thought. But the basic translations referred to are the Authorized Version and, especially, the Revised Standard Version.

The current spate of discussion about the Spirit is uncomfortably like a group of people in deep discussion about their pulse-rate, breathing and digestion. A bit hypochondriac. People in the full bloom of health haven't the same interest; they are too busy living. But there is some comfort. Often in writing this book I had the recurring feeling that what I was *really* talking about was the life of the Father and the Son in the hearts of those that love God. And that is how I would like it to be read.

JOHN PECK

1

THE SPIRIT

Not ideas, ideals, fine feelings, but happenings.

Readings: Genesis 1:2; Exodus 31:3; 1 Samuel 10:10; Joel 2:28; Matthew 1:18; 12:25; Luke 4:1; Romans 5:5; Ephesians 6:17; Acts 2:1; John 3:5; 7:17.

If you read through references in the Bible such as those in the list above, one thing will stand out straight away. It is just that wherever the Spirit of God is mentioned, *something is happening* as a result. Maybe not quite what people were expecting or hoping for, but still, almost always, something happening. Even in situations where this is not clearly the case, you usually get the feeling that there is tremendous power in the background, waiting to burst into action. In ordinary language we talk about the spirit of a meeting, or the spirit of a person, and we think of 'spirit' then as something rather like air or thought – not very solid, and not easily defined. And when we read in the New Testament about the 'Spirit of God in you', we tend to assume that this is what it means in practice. There is no doubt that God's Spirit can and does produce ideas in people, and atmospheres in meetings, but the Bible does not speak of him chiefly like that. In the Old Testament (and it was mainly from the Old Testament that writers like John and Paul got their basic notions of God) people might misunderstand *what* was happening when the Spirit was at work, but they were hardly ever in doubt that *something* was happening and it would be mighty hard to stop it! When Isaiah wanted to show how foolish it was for Israel to rely on military help from Egypt, he wrote, 'The Egyptians are only human, not God: their horses [the ancient world's equivalent of war-planes] are only flesh and *not spirit*' (that would be something to be really afraid of! – Isaiah 31:3).

The Old Testament's Hebrew word for 'Spirit' is *ruach* (pronounced *roo-ukh*, with the *kh* like the guttural ending to the Scots word 'loch' breathed forcefully). It is a fine word, full of power. Now the word also had simpler meanings – it could mean 'wind'. And though it was used for the fresh breeze that blew up at the end of a hot day (Genesis 3:8 is the 'ruach of the day'), by far the commonest forms of wind in that part of the world are hot, fierce, gusty and devastating.

The word could also mean 'breath'. But not quiet peaceful breathing that we are hardly aware of; there was another gentler word for that (*n'shama*). It meant the fast noisy breathing of a man in passion or in violent exertion – getting worked up for something to happen. Sometimes it is difficult to decide whether it should be translated 'wind' or 'spirit'; but if you think of it, any language in which 'God's Spirit' could equally mean God's stormwind, or 'God's violent breathing', obviously doesn't regard the Spirit of God as a baby puffing at a candle on a birthday cake.

In the beginning

The Spirit of God appears on the scene as soon as we open the Bible. He is there as soon as creation comes into being. The scene is painted in verse 2 of Genesis 1; confronting us with an empty, shapeless earth, and a universe like an astronomer's hole in space – in itself sterile and still. But there, across it, *something is happening*; there *is* movement and power: the Spirit of God 'moving ...' The word 'moving' is too sedate really. The original word was used of an eagle stirring up a nest of its young with the beating of its powerful wings. I don't think we have any word in English to combine the ideas of strength and constantly changing movement that this verse associates with the Spirit. Psalm 104 pictures it all even more vividly. Verse after verse speaks of the limitless variety and ingenuity of God's power, up to a climax in verses 27–32:

> Thou sendest forth thy Spirit, they are created.... He looks on the earth and it trembles; he touches the mountains, and they smoulder.

Actually, Psalm 104 goes rather further than Genesis 1:2. Not only was the Spirit of God at work bringing creation into being as we know it, but he is also at work keeping the whole thing going in all its manifold forms and variations.

So if we ask the question, 'What is the ultimate power behind the universe, behind the power of gravitation, the energy within the atom, the processes of germination, growth, animal life, consciousness?' then the Bible's answer is, not some refined force, but the Spirit of God. That means that the power by which creation is energized is not so much like the power of a wound-up spring, as like the effect of an overwhelmingly powerful personality.

We could make this issue even more pointed by asking the question, 'What is the power behind my *own* existence, whereby my own arm can move, my heart beat, my voice be heard?' And the answer would have to be the same: the Spirit of God. The possibility of turning any power that comes from such a source against God's will, and to use it in ways that disgrace him, is awesome and terrifying.

The beginning of man

The Book of Job is a poem that has many points of contact with the story of creation. In it Elihu, the last of Job's friends, insists that he is just as human as Job, and he puts it like this:

> The Spirit of God has made me
> And the breath of the Almighty has given me life.

Now Hebrew poetry does not use rhyming sounds, as we often do in English; instead it uses rhyming *ideas*. It appears here very clearly: 'Spirit of God' and 'breath of the Almighty' have similar meanings; so have 'made me' and 'given me life'. (Incidentally, it is interesting to see how well this goes over in translation: think how difficult it is to translate rhymes.)

The point of all this is that it gives us a clue to that rather strange verse in Genesis 2 (verse 7) – 'The LORD God formed man of the dust of the ground, and breathed into his nostrils the breath of life.' Job 33:4 (quoted above) shows us that the 'breath of God' was really another way here of saying that man was brought into being by the Spirit of God. Actually that in itself would be very remarkable, but there is more to it. A comparison with the way that animals were made shows up quite staggering differences. Of the animals, God said 'let there be . . .' and it was so. But with man, there seems to have been reflection within the Trinity before the final climax – 'Let us make man....' Then the actual process is described – a work of craftsmanship, forming man out of the dust. And finally God draws especially close (it is hard here not to think of a 'kiss of life') and he puts something into man from the depths of his own being. It is all so intimate.

The result of this very special act of God's spirit is to produce a creature which, for all that he is made of the same stuff as plants and animals, is quite different. He can be specially close to God. He has the power to *control* the world, not just survive in it. He can receive verbal instructions from God, and can make up words to identify things that he finds. He is actually 'made in God's image'. (Genesis 1:27, 2:15–17, 2:20ff.) Even his sexuality is something special – not just for reproduction, but fellowship. Now this power has never been revoked. Man has misused it, but he still has it. He makes tools, handles fire, plans a harvest, makes sound into music, makes rock and clay into buildings, harnesses electricity for his purposes, makes fibres into clothes, and so on. If we ask the question, 'How did God bring this about?' then the answer must be 'by the breath of the Almighty, the Spirit of God.'

There is more. God does not do things because he is forced to act, or because of some blind instinct. He *chooses* to act.

Continually through the Bible we read of God saying 'I will ..., I am ..., I will....' (A good example of this is in Exodus 3.) And he has given a power like that to man. It is only man that chooses whether to obey or disobey God's commands such as the one in Genesis 2:17. Only God's Spirit could make a being in God's image like that. Again, the possibility of turning such a power against the Creator is awesome. And yet there are texts that speak of it – a struggle between God and man (Genesis 6:3; Isaiah 53:10; Acts 7:51). And human history gives evidence of it. It is horrific: like making a sinister parody of a picture of a loved one. Or, perhaps skewering an effigy on a gibbet ...

All this adds up to the fact that nothing that ever happens anywhere in the universe or in man himself, does so without the Spirit of God. And this is a fact whether human beings recognize it or not.

As a matter of fact, the Bible does not make very much of the activity of the Spirit in creation at large. There are only a handful of texts about it, and the scholars argue about the meaning of some of these. The teaching comes not just from the texts, however, but from the fact that the Bible speaks of creation as the work of God as Father and God as Son, and it would be very strange to reject the idea of the Spirit at work in the face of an ordinary and natural understanding of the texts we have considered.

But the Bible's main interest in the Spirit's work is elsewhere. His work in creation is foundational, on which the main structure of teaching is built. And one does not expect, after all, to see much of a building's foundations. The Bible's main interest in the work of the Spirit is in man's relationship to God.

The Spirit, man, and God

The Prophets

We start once more with the Old Testament as giving us the basic ideas for the New. A study of the Old Testament references to 'Spirit' in a concordance soon shows up an interesting fact.

Most of the references are about one particular work of the Spirit: that of inspiring prophets. Now prophets were not just crystal-gazers. They were people whose whole being was involved in their message. Much of their behaviour would seem very strange to westerners today. Ezekiel speaks a good deal about the power of the spirit in his life, and some very strange things happened. On one occasion he seems to have experienced a kind of levitation along with a powerful emotional disturbance (Ezekiel 3:14 and elsewhere). Sometimes he had remarkable visions (e.g. 8:3). By Ezekiel's time that sort of thing seems to have been a bit suspect, because false prophets could work up some experiences to deceive people. But in Samuel's time, some 500 years before, it was a common thing among the prophets; it was even, in a way, catching! Saul, apparently a very unlikely candidate for such things, on one occasion comes under the influence of a band of such prophets, and the neighbours said, 'What's come over the son of Kish?' (1 Samuel 10:6–13). The Spirit could take people over in spite of themselves. On a later occasion this happened to some of Saul's hoodlums who were sent to capture David. The whole affair must have been highly embarrassing and Saul himself was once again involved (1 Samuel 19:18–24).

The idea of the Spirit producing effects of a power that can be unmistakably felt is still very much to the fore.

These rather bizarre manifestations (as we may think) tended to get less frequent among the great prophets. But there is evidence that they never completely lost what we might call ecstatic experiences. If we go back to the ancient example of Balaam in Numbers 23 and 24, it is obvious there that the effect of the Spirit was to make him speak in a cryptic kind of poetry, rather like an incantation. And right the way through the Old Testament we get the same thing: most of the prophets utter their oracles in a style rather like this. It appears, too, in the New Testament – Luke's account of the outburst of prophecy which came at the time of Christ's birth gives us the prophetic songs that are still sung in some churches – the 'Magnificat', the 'Benedictus' and the 'Nunc Dimittis' (see

Luke 1 and 2). Even Jesus seems to have had a similar experience in Luke 10:21; where, rejoicing 'in the Holy Spirit', he speaks to God in a 'high' style of language, and then seems to 'come down to earth' when he turns to his disciples in verse 23.

What does happen, however, is that the Spirit of God took over more and more of the *lives* of the prophets. Ecstatic experiences may come and go – indeed some people seem to be able to turn them on or off at will. But the great prophets of the Old Testament found that the Spirit of God tended to take them over in experiences that had long-lasting effects. Sometimes very long-lasting indeed. Elijah, for instance, found that God was sending him from place to place to speak and work for him. Amos was not even trained to be a prophet, as most leading prophets were; and his whole pattern of life as a farm-worker was changed. Being a prophet for Hosea was a heart-rending business – involving him in the agonizing struggle to win back a wayward wife. So we could go on: Isaiah's children, Ezekiel's loss of his wife, and Habakkuk's theological problems are other examples. Sometimes it seems that the very bodily presence of the prophet was part of his prophecy – Jeremiah, for instance, in calling for spiritual realism when Jerusalem was on the point of collapse, was questioned and criticized and threatened and appealed to and imprisoned and released – no one seemed to know what to do with him! What happens, in effect, is that where the Spirit worked in this special way, *anything* in a man's life could carry God's message to others, not simply what he said.

The Spirit and Jesus Christ

All this sounds like a pretty devastating total involvement. But when we go into the New Testament, we find an example there which makes even the greatest of the Old Testament prophets look like amateurs. For a man appears on the scene whose very birth comes about by the Spirit. His entry into public life is marked by a visible descent of the Spirit (Luke 3:22; John 1:33).

The crowds called Jesus a prophet, but the writer to the Hebrews said far more (Hebrews 1:1):

> God, who in many and various ways spoke of old to our fathers by the prophets, has in these last days spoken to us by – a Son.

At last the Spirit of God has a man whose entire being is a message from God. As John puts it he is God's word made flesh.

Paul speaks of Christ's rising from the dead as connected with the Spirit. In one striking passage, looking at Christ's presence as a whole in human history, he calls him 'the last Adam', and says he 'became a life-giving spirit'. All this will need more detailed treatment later. At this point, the reference to the resurrection draws our attention to another aspect of the Spirit's work.

The Life-giving Spirit:

When God created man, according to the account in Genesis 2, he 'breathed into his nostrils the breath of life, and man became a living soul,' (verse 7). This seems pretty clearly a way of saying that man received his life by the Spirit. But the matter did not end there because man's sin 'brought death into the world'. A burning question then arises, which Job, in the depths of his anguish, expressed quite simply, 'if a man die, can he live again?' (Job 14:14). Like the growing light of a dawn, the Bible's triumphant answer is 'Yes!' It appears in the Old Testament as something fitful and rather ambiguous to begin with. The prophets seem to have felt it first of all (at least in ways that we would recognize today) when they looked at God's people devastated by disaster, and a land strewn with dead, which were really but symptoms and symbols of something far worse – a death of a nation's morale, of its contact with God. Maybe strange miracles of the past, like the raising of man whose body touched Elisha's bones (2 Kings 13:21) may have helped. Anyway, Isaiah, out of the depths of gloom, found it possible to say 'Thy dead shall live . . .' (Isaiah 26:19). And in a mysterious way, Isaiah speaks of a Servant of the Lord who would die,

and yet at least live enough to be satisfied with the results of
his death and its agonies (Isaiah 53:9–11).

How could such a thing be? Well, the nation had to 'die'
a death more final than anything Isaiah knew for such a vision
to be possible. Ezekiel, a captive exile even before Jerusalem
was reduced to rubble by Nebuchadnezzar in 586 B.C., spoke
of a resurrection of his people (Ezekiel 36 and 37). And he saw
it coming about by the Spirit of God. God would come into
a new relationship with his people – a new 'covenant'. It would
involve giving life to men's hearts, as it were from dead stone
to living flesh. He utters the word from God: 'I will put my
spirit within you,' (Ezekiel 36:27). In the next chapter he has
a vision of the remains of a battlefield long neglected – the
slain lie in the valley as 'dry bones'. *Very* dry. And by the
word of prophecy and the blowing of God's wind, they are
remade as living men – 'an exceeding great army'. It is difficult to know whether Ezekiel took this literally as meaning that
Israel's past dead would come back to life; perhaps we ought
not to try to pin him down too closely. But the Bible tends
to be disturbingly *physical* in its concerns, and I doubt whether
bodily resurrection could have been quite ruled out. The point
is that in this very symbolic passage we come up against an
unmistakable symbol for the Spirit – that is, the wind (37:8–10).
In fact, the Hebrew word is our old friend *ruach*. It is the
Spirit who gives life to the dead, and from the dead. (With
this sort of vision before him, we can understand the confidence
of Daniel as he sees the End (Daniel 12) when all men shall
rise from the dust of death.)

In the New Testament the picture is much clearer. As Paul
says (2 Timothy 1:10), Christ 'brought life and immortality to
light through the gospel'. On the whole, the New Testament
still sees this new life from the two points of view: heart and
body. But whichever point of view is referred to, new life comes
into being by the Spirit. Those who trust in Jesus Christ are
reborn – born from above – by the Spirit (John 3:8) which
blows like the wind. Perhaps Jesus had Ezekiel 37 in mind.
To the Corinthian Christians (1 Corinthians 15:45) Paul says

that Christ, in contrast with Adam, stands for a 'life-giving Spirit'. In his great panorama of salvation in Romans, Paul says that the 'law of the Spirit of life in Christ Jesus has set me free from the law of sin and death' (Romans 8:2). But those whose *hearts* are made alive will also have their bodily life renewed as well – 'If the Spirit ... dwells in you, [God] will give life to your mortal bodies by his spirit...' (Romans 8:11). Once again we are confronted with power on an immense scale, producing results far beyond the capabilities of any human science.

There is a distinct change of emphasis in passing from the Old Testament to the New, and this can be deceptive. Almost all the Old Testament references to the Spirit speak of him as acting on people, in a way, from *outside* of their ordinary life, invading it, so to speak. So the Spirit 'fell upon' Ezekiel for example, and the Spirit takes over Gideon like a suit of clothes (Ezekiel 11–5; Judges 6–34; Hebrew). The effect could be rather like that of an electric current, or a lightning stroke, or a storm blowing, or the mass-psychology of a crowd. But in the New Testament, especially in the epistles, the emphasis is on something happening deep within the personality. Paul says, for instance, that 'the love of God is poured forth into our hearts by the Holy Spirit which is given to us' (Romans 5:5). In Romans 8:1–11 the main emphasis is on the Holy Spirit 'dwelling within you'.

In the letter to the Hebrews, a book very obviously under Old Testament inspiration, the difference is even spelled out: 'The Holy Spirit bears witness to us: "... I will put my laws on their hearts, and write them on their minds ..."' (Hebrews 10:15–16).

In John's writings, everywhere you go it is uppermost. Going on from John 3 to John 7:37–39 you find the idea, not just of the Spirit indwelling, but of the Spirit overflowing, giving life to all around. In Jesus's last words to his disciples before the cross, he promises 'the Spirit of truth ... He dwells with you, and *shall be in you*.' There is almost a suggestion that through-out the Old Testament, the Spirit of God was waiting to make

himself really at home in a man's life. It happened in Jesus
Christ; and that gave him an opening: from then on, anyone
who might belong to Jesus Christ would find the Spirit actually
permanently at work in his thinking and feeling, his wishing
and planning, and his praying, hoping, learning, looking and
loving.

After his resurrection, there is an incident mentioned in John
20:22 in which Jesus breathes on the disciples, and says 'Receive
the Holy Spirit. . . .' Now there are many places in John's gospel
where John seems to see what is happening as a kind of new
version of Genesis (compare John 1:1 with Genesis 1:1; John
8:12 and 12:46 with Genesis 1:3; his phrase 'from the beginning'
(especially John 8:44); and 18:1 with the garden in Genesis 2
and 3). This looks like another of these. It is as if Jesus is doing
for the new life what God did to Adam in giving him the first.
It is the same idea as we glanced at in 1 Corinthians 15:45.
But this is only preparatory, surely, to the great event of Pentecost, when the Spirit of prophecy and the Spirit of resurrection
life comes down through the infant church to all mankind.

I said that this was deceptive. It is so, because without the
Old Testament ideas to stand on, we would easily slide into
the notion that the Spirit of God is just about feelings, ideas,
atmospheres of thought, in which nothing necessarily gets *done*.
This is far from the truth. The Spirit of God works on the
heart first of all. And in the Bible 'the heart' does not mean
thought, so much as what does the thinking; not so much
emotion, as motivation. It is about that part of us that holds
the helm, that fixes our choice on a guiding star. It is what
governs the hidden driving passions of our life, the power in
us which makes for decision and action. To get at *that* requires
a degree of power greater than anything which (in the realm
of physics) probes the interior of the atom or the depths of
space. And it would be inconceivable to anyone living in the
world of the Bible that such power could be at work without
results that would show up in all directions. Granted that people
might not understand, or might misunderstand. Granted that
those whose hearts are changed might be unaware of the effects

on those around them, just as Moses, bearing less glory in the Old Testament, did not realize that his face shone (Exodus 34:29). People might well offer wrong explanations, as they did at Pentecost when they said the disciples had had too much fresh wine (Acts 2:13). But read Peter's quotation from Joel on what would happen when the Spirit came (Acts 2:17–21). Then imagine yourself saying to Peter, 'The Spirit was present in our meeting last night. Nothing very dramatic, you understand. Just a deep feeling of peace. It seems such a shame to have to come down to the same old life afterwards.' Surely, if you caught him in the right mood, he would just fall about laughing. Explanations might be mistaken, but one thing is sure, that when the Spirit of the Lord was at work in the world of the Bible, things would happen in people's lives that would cry out for *some* sort of explanation!

2

THE SPIRIT OF FAITH

Not just any experiences, but experiences of faith.

Readings: Ezekiel 36:26–27; Joel 2:28–29; John 3:5–16; John 16:7–15;
Galatians 3:1–5; 1 John 3:24 – 4:6.

I remember once being engaged in the work of following up
an evangelistic campaign in a church where there had been a
large number of professed conversions. I found the task rather
bewildering. Time and time again I had conversations which
went rather like this:

'So you become a Christian, then, at the campaign?'

'Yes.'

'That's wonderful! Do tell me what happened.'

'Well, this man was preaching, and at the end he asked any-
body who wanted to to come forward, and I felt I had to, so
I did.'

'So what happened then?'

'Well, he talked to me a bit, and then we had a prayer, and
I signed a card.'

'And what happened after that?'

'What do you mean?'

'Well, what happened in your life?'

'Well, nothing very much. I started to come to church, of
course.'

'Why was that?'

'I don't know really. I mean, you're supposed to come to
church, aren't you?'

'Yes ... what actually made you go forward at the appeal?'
'I don't know really. Just some sort of urge. I just had to.'
'So the man then told you about Jesus Christ?'
'I suppose he must have. I can't really remember.'
'Well, what did you do when he prayed with you?'
'Nothing in particular. But he was very nice.'
'Do you feel that your life has changed since?'
'I don't know ...'

And I could get no further. The whole affair was well described by someone who taught me a great deal about evangelism as a message of 'I've had an experience, come to the front and you can have an experience.'

When the Bible speaks of the Spirit of God in a person's experience, it does not mean *any* kind of experience. The Spirit of God is basically concerned in Scripture with the experience of faith. So Paul speaks of the Spirit as 'the Spirit of faith' (2 Corinthians 4:13). The Spirit is the source of the whole life-experience of the believer, as appears from Galatians 5:22 – 'the fruit of the Spirit is love, joy, peace, longsuffering, kindness, goodness, faithfulness, gentleness, self-control.' But these are all derived from faith. Earlier in the chapter Paul makes this clear (verse 5) when he says, 'for through the Spirit, by faith, we wait for the hope of righteousness.'

Facing God as real

'Faith' itself is a word that needs careful consideration. It is not, as one writer described the screen version of it, 'a yearn in soft focus'. Nor is it simply belief, assent to a proposition, or the adoption of a religious way of life. When, in the Bible, people put their faith in God, the outstanding thing is the way in which God is a reality for them as they do it. It is this which makes true faith.

Consider the following as an illustration. A lot is said these days about fire precautions. Lecturers can be asked to come and give instruction about it. Now undoubtedly a man who has studied the behaviour of fires all over the world would be able to give us a great deal of help. So would a fireman, who, even without actually having been to a fire, had been thoroughly trained in all the procedures involved in fighting one. No doubt a poet with a vivid imagination would be able to help us to feel the horror of it. But it would be quite another matter if we began to smell smoke in the room, and hear the crackle of flames! Put simply, the difference is that in the last case, and that only, there is no option about responding to the situation. We would have to do something about the fire – we would have to take it seriously. What before was a matter for interest, consideration, discussion, or even precautionary action, now becomes an immediate pressing reality. The 'faith' which is the work of the Spirit is a response which arises out of the fact that God has become a pressing reality.

The parable of the fire is an appropriate one in a way, because God is actually spoken of as a 'consuming fire' in the Bible (Hebrews 12:29, cf. Deuteronomy 4:24), and it is also one of the symbols of the Spirit (Acts 2:3). But it could also be a little misleading, because the Bible does use other, less spectacular picture-language for God, like anointing oil (e.g. Acts 10:38) and 'a whisper of gentle stillness' (1 Kings 19:12). In fact, in that last reference, it is expressly said that on that particular occasion that 'the LORD was not in the fire'. But the point is that God becomes a reality in people's experience by the Spirit, whatever the particular experience may be at the time. And it is this which makes faith possible. What happened as a result will vary. If you know that your life is not right, but you have got so used to the idea that it doesn't matter any more, then obviously such an experience is going to be very disturbing; you'll see things in a very different light. If a person has been very muddled in his thinking about God, then his thinking is going to alter, especially if he has been generally of the opinion that there is no such Being. You then have to make up your mind whether to accept the implications or not. If you accept them, there will be a change of attitude on a very deep level.

This change of attitude is an aspect of the faith experience which the Bible calls 'repentance'. It is most to the fore in the synoptic gospels (e.g. Matthew 9:13; 21:29; Mark 1:15; Luke 13:3; 15:7; 24:47). On the other hand, in John's gospel the word is not used at all. This is because when John uses words like 'faith' and 'believe' he takes it for granted that repentance is included. And he refers to this aspect of the Spirit's work in citing Jesus's own words at the last supper: 'He shall convince the world of sin ...' (John 16:8–11). Such an experience of God is impossible unless he is a reality by the Spirit; and we can begin to appreciate that rather strange remark of Peter and the others to the High Priest when they were charged with subversive activity: 'God exalted him [Jesus] to *give* repentance to Israel ...' (Acts 5:31, cf. 11:18).

Something outside ourselves

We need to think through this idea of God in our experience, because confusion is disturbingly common, and the conversation at the beginning of this chapter is a typical example. It is only too easy for us to talk of an experience of faith as if it were something that only goes on inside the mind or feelings, especially if there is no visible cause for it.

The fact is that we have two kinds of experience in life. One kind is the sort that goes on entirely within our own mental processes. For instance we may be faced with a problem which has teased us to a standstill. Then, perhaps the next morning, the solution occurs to us. A different example of this sort of experience would be that of a dream.

The other kind of experience is aroused by something outside us, like hearing a voice or bumping into a lamp-post. For a sane life these two kinds of experience have to interact. If all our living were simply reacting to our environment, we would at best be no better than animals. We need the inner experience of imagination and reasoned thinking as well. But these need monitoring: they have to be checked against the outside world. The outside world, for instance, soon resists any tendency I might have to think I am Billy Graham or Napoleon.

The trouble with experiences of God is that there is,

apparently, no 'outside world' by which I can run a check; the whole thing is his anyway – there is, so to speak, no independent evidence. This makes it only too easy to think of experiencing God as the same sort of experience as that of an emotional upheaval, or of arriving at a decision in one's own mind, or even of a dream. But this is not the case. The Spirit of God brings us face to face with God as someone very distinctly *not* of our own feelings and thinking, but as someone 'beyond' us, 'above' us; someone whose attitudes are not the same as ours. It is a curious experience; rather like being confronted with an artistic masterpiece. We could never have imagined it like that; and yet, having seen it, we could never imagine it any different. There is often conflict, especially if we stand to lose rather heavily by accepting the implications of meeting God in this way. But there are no alternatives worth considering.

Faith directs us away from ourselves

This fact, that the experience of faith which the Spirit brings is of 'something outside' a man, means that the person concerned tends to get taken up not so much with the experience as with the cause of it. If I crack my shins on a low table in a dark room I am liable to say 'Ouch!' and rub my shin; and almost in the same breath to say 'what on earth is that?' And when the pain has subsided, I investigate, and maybe move the offending furniture. The person who meets God will certainly feel it as an experience, but he will inevitably go on to say something like 'who in heaven is that?' and then get absorbed in dealing with God.

There is an interesting example of this process in the account of the infant church in Acts. The first half of the book is full of references to the Holy Spirit, his gifts of power and wisdom and love; in the second half he is barely mentioned. Now it was not that the Spirit had stopped working, but that the Christians were less occupied with their inner experience (that is, the Spirit) and more absorbed with God as the one who had caused it. In this respect the Spirit functions like a pair of spectacles. When someone has spectacles for the first time, two things will happen. One is that he gets a clearer vision of the world around him. The other is that he will probably be very much aware of the glasses on his nose. Now in fact this awareness is actually a distraction from perfect vision, but it cannot be helped, and gradually he gets used to them. But getting used to them never means that he can do without them, it just means that they are no longer in the forefront of his thoughts. The lenses in fact have no colours or outlines; they exist solely to enable the wearer to be aware of what he can see through them. So Christ said of the Spirit, 'he will not speak on his own authority, but whatever he hears he will speak, ... He will glorify me,' (John 16:13–14).

Faith and miracles

Earlier I made the remark that the experience of God cannot be 'monitored' by evidence from the world of the senses. That is not entirely true. One of the remarkable things about the gospel is that it speaks of a God who reveals himself in the material circumstances of life. Jesus Christ himself was God in human flesh. The early apostles spoke of their message as being attested by the 'demonstration of the Spirit and power' (1 Corinthians 2:4) with 'signs and wonders (Acts 14:3; Romans 15:19; Hebrews 2:4). Jesus himself at one point had said to his disciples, 'Believe me for the very works' sake,' (John 14:11). In other words, just as Jesus performed miracles during his life on earth, so the Spirit performed them through the apostles, and to a certain extent these were aids to faith. And though the Christian church has sometimes been very sceptical about miracles, the fact remains that such things have been happening ever since.

But the Bible itself has a curiously mixed attitude towards miracles. Christ himself kept doing them, but he also kept telling people not to advertise them (Mark 7:24, 36; 8:26), and they were frequently played down (cf. John 6:26, Mark 8:12).

The reason for this is connected with the whole nature of the Spirit's work. The trouble with miracles is that they tend to be too spectacular Human beings tend to attach too much importance to the world they can see and touch. When people are out of touch with God, this world is all there is to live by. So when they have some experience of this kind, they tend to become over-absorbed by it. But the Spirit is always pointing beyond the experience to God.

There is another, related snag about miracles: although they look as if they should prove something conclusively, in fact they never do. Jesus said, 'Many will come and say unto me, "Lord, Lord, ... have we not done miracles in your name?" And I will say to them, I never knew you.' (Matthew 7:22–23.) Strange things can be done by the devotees of other religions, and they too could be called miracles. Pharaoh's magicians could at least be a challenge to Moses in this respect, even if an unsuccessful one (Exodus 7:11–12). So what use are miracles?

There are three words used in the New Testament for a miracle, which could give some clues. One word is the Greek word *teras* (more often in the plural, *terata*), generally translated 'wonder'. Another word is *dynamis* (from which our word 'dynamite' comes, which stresses the fact that power or energy was at work in a miracle). The third word is *semeion* (from which the word 'semantics' comes – the study of meaning) which meant 'a sign'. This is specially important because it means that the Spirit's miracles are never just gimmicks or magical tricks. Nor do they exist just to get human beings out of difficulty.

A good example of how a miracle works is found in Exodus 3, the story of the burning bush.

Sometimes, apparently, dried shrubbery does momentarily burst into flame in the intense heat of the desert, but the fire does not last for long. So this particular event shows God's power; it is a *dynamis*. But it is also extraordinary, a *teras*. Moses' reaction was exactly what a *teras* should produce – 'I will now turn aside....' (Obviously if people are too self-absorbed, or are so sure that the universe has no mysteries, this would not happen.) So the miracle makes it possible for Moses to become aware of God's presence. But the fire in the bush was not only something remarkable; it also carried a symbolic meaning; it was a *semeion*. Fire was a symbol of God: to those who treated it with respect, it was a blessing; but to the casual and careless it was devastatingly destructive. The bush was to be a reminder for all of history of the possibility of God's becoming present in all his power in human life, without that life being destroyed.

The work of the Spirit in men's lives may from time to time be associated with miracles, because where he is at work, there is power, physical as well as mental and moral power. But this work of the Spirit, making people sure of God, does not depend on miracles. They act as warning lights, signposts, flashing indicators on the road of life. They are not proofs of God, only evidence – symptoms of his presence. They make faith a possibility, but they will never make unbelief impossible. Since God is the Creator of all things, miracles give a hint of the power that made the universe. Since man has marred God's creation, and Christ died to redeem it, miracles give a hint of how one day the whole creation will be healed, rebuilt, cleansed, and brought to new life.

Faith does not depend on sense-experience. The kind of faith which the Spirit gives cannot depend on anything that we can see or handle or feel. Certainty about anything always depends on a proof that is appropriate to it. The proof of a pudding is in the eating. The proof of a claim made for, say, two million puddings, is not just by eating – there's no stomach big enough! For this we have to introduce a process of reasoning, such as an argument based on the idea that if the same recipe and cooking method is used, then one pudding will taste like another. We accept this so naturally that we hardly realize we have shifted from one method to another of being able to have faith in a certain pudding. But we do it all the time. The larger the subject for proof, the larger the means needed to obtain it.

So what sort of thing is going to be 'large' enough to make

us sure of God? To ask for a certainty about God which depends on our senses, or our feelings, or our reason (and that is what people usually mean by saying 'prove there is a God') is like insisting that we won't buy any one of a batch of two million puddings until we have tasted them all! The kind of faith we are dealing with here is one which is only possible when God is personally present in our lives. It is, actually, a matter of real difficulty for us. The Spirit may make God a reality, and the result of that is a very definite experience – of joy, fear, regret, resolution, awe or action, or whatever. And because we are so in the habit of testing things by human experience, we easily slip into thinking that it is the experience itself which makes God's presence a certainty. And the next thing is that when we don't have that particular experience, we aren't sure of God any more....

The Spirit and faith

To live in the Spirit means to live by faith. To live by faith is to experience God. To experience God is to trust God whether we are 'having experiences' of him or not. There is a deep paradox here. Saints throughout the ages have borne witness to the fact that the profoundest faith-experience of God feels, at the time, like an experience of his absence. C. S. Lewis expresses it powerfully when, in *Screwtape Letters*, he makes the demon Screwtape write

> 'Our cause is never more in danger than when a human, no longer desiring, but still intending, to do our Enemy's will, looks round upon a universe from which every trace of him seems to have vanished, and asks why he has been forsaken, and still obeys.' (Screwtape Letters VIII, Collins/Fount.)

I have spent some time on the subject of miracles because they are so easily misunderstood. And, in a way, even now something more needs to be said. Because to describe miracles as merely signs and symptoms sounds rather cold and clinical, especially to anyone who has just been in the middle of one.

The fact is that there is one miracle which is really the pattern, the prototype of all God's miracles – that is, the presence of God in the world as the 'man Christ Jesus'. Here is God's power at work; here is God calling us to take notice of him; here God gives us the supreme 'sign' of what he is really like. When someone really 'turns aside to see this great sight', and really seeks to find out about Jesus, then the Spirit makes God a reality to him. The Spirit of God is not the spirit of any sort of 'god' – Muslim, Hindu, Christian Scientist, or whatever. He is the Spirit of Christ.

3

THE SPIRIT OF CHRIST

The Spirit brings experience of God; not as some vague supernatural being, but one with the nature and character of Jesus Christ.

Readings: 1 John 4; Luke 1; John 3:1–16; Romans 6:1–11; Romans 8:1–17.

There is a quite common idea that if a person has some powerful spiritual experience, no matter what notions of God are carried within it, then this is the work of the Holy Spirit, and what has been discovered in such an experience is automatically to be accepted as truth. This idea is reinforced if the person concerned is a professing Christian.

But the Bible does not teach this. The New Testament letters were addressed to Christians, largely about the way things should go on in their own church life. But when Paul is giving some final advice in the first letter to the Thessalonians, he says, 'Do not quench the Spirit, do not despise prophesying, but test everything,' (1 Thessalonians 5:19–20). Prophesying was, of course, a very characteristic experience of the Holy Spirit. But Paul's idea of showing respect for it was not to accept it without question, but to *test it every time*. Similarly, John in 1 John 4:1, says that we are to 'test the spirits whether they are of God'. Obviously then, as far as the Bible is concerned, it was possible to have misleading spiritual experiences. Paul even goes so far in one place as to say 'even Satan disguises himself as an angel of light' (2 Corinthians 11:14). We also need to remember that at least some spiritual experiences do not carry a meaning at all unless they are interpreted, and some can be disastrously misinterpreted. Nebuchadnezzar had a dream, which was clearly a spiritual experience (Daniel 4); but·it took a Daniel 'in whom is the spirit of the holy God' (4:18) to interpret it. Paul says that the presence of himself and his fellow evangelists brought a spiritual experience to those with whom they came in contact: they brought the 'scent' of Christ to people (2 Corinthians 2:14). But he goes on to say that to some, who took it wrongly, it was 'the scent of death'.

So the question arises, what kind of spiritual experience is the kind brought about by the Spirit? What is the vision of God which is characteristic of him?

First and foremost, the Spirit is the Spirit of Christ. Whatever other tests might be applied, says Paul, this much is certainly true, that 'no one speaking by the Spirit of God ever says "Jesus be cursed"' (1 Corinthians 12:3). The God presented to us by the Holy Spirit is not just some Mighty Being to inspire a sense of awe or a feeling of love. He is the God and Father of our Lord Jesus Christ.

The Spirit in non-Christian religions

It would be best to deal with an issue here which otherwise may drag at our feet through to the last page. If the Holy Spirit is the Spirit of Christ, and only that, does this mean that there is nothing good in other religions, that all their spiritual experiences have no value at all?

No, it does not. The issues behind this subject are too vast to be dealt with in this book, but this much can be said. Paul says that the Gentiles (that is, all those who are without the revelation given to God's people) 'hold the truth in unrighteousness' (Romans 1:18 AV). It is not that they do not have the truth, but that the perversity of the human heart suppresses it, weakens and distorts its meaning in such a way that unaided man cannot distinguish it clearly from falsehood. For example, some religions teach quite strongly the idea of God's love, even to saying as John does (1 John 4:8) that 'God is love'. It looks as if we all agree at this point. But in fact we find that their concept of 'love' is modelled on some human experience of friendship, or marriage, or emotional ecstasy, all of which are only seen tainted by human sin. The result is a confused and muddled doctrine. That is because such forms of love only find their fullest meaning when they develop under the cleansing power of a still higher kind of love altogether. John goes on to say: 'herein is love, ... that God sent his Son to be the propitiation for our sins.' (1 John 4:10.) In other words a doctrine of God's love only means what it ought to mean when we expound it in terms of Christ and his death on Calvary for sin.

This is why we cannot regard other religions as if these were options having equality with the gospel of Christ. We do not say that there is no activity of the Spirit in other religions, but the Bible insists that what he is doing is always to urge men to 'seek after God'; a God who can only be found in Jesus Christ (Acts 14:15; 17:23–31). Christians can indeed learn from other religions, for they may well find truths in a garbled form that they have overlooked or forgotten. The fact is that only Christians *can* learn from other religions, for only through Christ can truth be identified in the midst of error. And the reverse is true: non-Christians cannot learn the truth about God from *any* religion until they have first found him in Jesus Christ. So Paul on Mars Hill takes a truth common in heathen religion – the notion that there is a Being who is the source of all that exists. In the pagan world, such a being is essentially unknowable: he is the 'unknown God'. But such a notion makes the belief in a Creator a completely useless idea for practical godly living – it 'holds down the truth in unrighteousness'. Paul, however, puts the truth in its right context – he goes on to say that the God whom they ignorantly worship has made himself known to mankind by one man in particular, whom he raised from the dead (Acts 17:22–31).

So everywhere in the world there is a sense in which the Spirit does give man truth, but man cannot recognize it or

appreciate it unless he finds Jesus Christ, who is *the* truth. Man
is like someone with a jigsaw puzzle to make up; but some of
the pieces he has belong to another jigsaw, and he has no
picture to guide him. The picture is Christ. Those who know
him can recognize what is truly his anywhere in the world.

The Spirit in Christ's earthly life

The Spirit of God, then, is the Spirit of Christ. We can begin
to consider this fact first of all by looking at the way the Spirit
worked in the earthly life of Jesus Christ. For this, let us go
first of all to the gospels. And straight away a principle we have
already noticed is found to be at work. On the whole there are
surprisingly few references to the Spirit in comparison with,
say, the letters of Paul. The bulk of them cluster round two
great events – his birth and his baptism. This is because the
Spirit always goes off-stage once he has done his work of
introducing Jesus Christ. Elsewhere in the gospels, the
references to the Spirit are as it were kept to the barest
minimum; and in a way that makes them all the more significant.

Certainly at Jesus's entry into the world the Spirit is very
much in evidence. As if to herald a royal visitation, there is
what has been called 'an outburst of prophecy'. Now, this was
remarkable because for centuries there had been no prophets
among the Jews, and as we have seen, the Old Testament
regarded prophecy as in a very special way the work of God's
spirit. The prophet Joel had foretold a day when the Spirit
would be poured out 'on all flesh', upon even 'menservants and
maidservants' (Joel 2:28–29), so that all sorts of quite ordinary
people would act as prophets. And this was to be the sign of
the New Age, when God would come to put the world to rights.
For centuries the Jews had been waiting for this promise to
be fulfilled. Then the silence is broken.

A devout priest name Zechariah has a prophetic vision in
the temple. The message speaks of a child to be born who would
be in the line of the old prophets – called from his mother's

womb, like Jeremiah, with the spirit and power of Elijah, carrying out the task of conversion spoken of in the last verses of the Old Testament (Malachi 4:5–6). Above all, he is to be 'filled with the Holy Spirit' (Luke 1:14–17). When Zechariah emerges from the temple, he is struck dumb, and people might well be reminded of what happened to the prophet Ezekiel (Ezekiel 3:26).

Some six months later, the same Spirit is spoken of as coming upon one 'maidservant of the Lord' in particular. This time the result is not simply words of prophecy, but the very source of all prophecy himself; the one who was the Word, the Son of God. (Luke 1:35; Matthew 1:18, 20; compare Hebrews 1:1–2.) And then for a while it seems that almost everywhere Mary went, people prophesied in the Spirit. Elizabeth, Zechariah's wife, bursts into prophecy; Mary herself prophesies; Zechariah prophesies; and then when the infant Jesus is presented at the temple, Simeon 'inspired by the Spirit' prophesies, and then Anna. (Luke 1 and 2.)

Nearly thirty years pass before the Spirit is referred to again; this time it is at the beginning of Jesus's public ministry. John the Baptist, Spirit-filled child of Elizabeth and Zechariah, is preaching in the desert near the ford of the Jordan. He is announcing the presence of someone who would baptize 'with the Holy Spirit and with fire' (Matthew 3:11; Mark 1:8; Luke 3:16; John 1:33).

And then Jesus comes to be baptized. The whole scene is traumatic for John. For one thing, he intuitively knows that this man does not need to repent and be baptized, yet he has to go through with it. For another thing, he has long had at the back of his mind the realization that one day someone would come on the scene who would be visibly anointed with the Holy Spirit; and this would be the man the world had been waiting for. When Jesus was baptized the Spirit came upon him, not simply as a power that could be detected by its effects, but actually in physical visible form, like a dove descending upon him (Luke 3:22).

From that point the Spirit goes to work in Jesus's life in a special way. He 'drives' Jesus into the desert to undergo conflict and testing (Mark 1:12); and Luke tells us that this was not just a temporary on-rush of the Spirit; it was the result of a permanent condition of Jesus's life – being 'full of the Holy Spirit' (Luke 4:1). This testing seems to have meant that the Spirit then gave him new resources of power – Luke says that he 'returned in the power of the Spirit into Galilee' to begin his ministry (Luke 4:14). When Jesus reached Nazareth and taught in the synagogue there, he made it quite clear that he himself saw his ministry in this light; for he claimed that the promise of Isaiah 61:1–2 applied to him: 'The Spirit of the Lord is upon me. . . .' His fellow townsmen knew full well what he was getting at, and reacted violently (Luke 4:28–30).

From then on references to the Spirit in the life of Jesus are relatively few; but the course has already been set. What has been said tells us that the whole of Jesus's ministry was done in the power of the Spirit. When John says that God does not give the Spirit 'by measure' to Jesus (3:34), it probably means that there was no limit at all to the power and presence of the Spirit in his life; that whenever you were confronted with Jesus, you felt the full impact of the Spirit. This gives a new force to Jesus's own claim in John 6:63 – 'It is the Spirit that gives life ... the words that I have spoken to you *are* [not just *have*] spirit and life.' The casual way in which Jesus is said after his resurrection to have 'given commandment by the Holy Spirit' (Acts 1:2) shows how completely Christ's life as a teacher was bound up with the Holy Spirit. There was absolutely nothing that he did and said of which you could not equally truly say that the Holy Spirit said and did it. The gospels tell us that he cast out demons by the Holy Spirit (Matthew 12:28). Even his inner experience could be spoken of as the working of the Spirit. In Luke 10:21 Jesus 'rejoiced in the Holy Spirit' at the way God was using simple people to spread his message. Other texts may indicate the same idea; for instance when Jesus stood before the tomb of Lazarus he 'groaned in spirit' (John 11:33). It is hard to tell whether this is referring to Jesus's inner human feelings or to the Holy Spirit. The fact that the

New Testament writers do not feel the need to make any clear distinction suggests that they may not have felt that there was one! If that is so then Hebrews 9:14 is especially interesting. This says that Christ 'through the eternal Spirit offered himself without blemish to God' (RSV and most other translations, although not NEB or Barclay). Certainly there is more than a hint that the Spirit of God was at work in the very climax of our redemption.

When we come to the resurrection of Christ, the scriptures several times associate this with the Holy Spirit (Romans 8:11; 1 Timothy 3:16; 1 Peter 3:18). And to complete the story is the fact that all the gifts and graces bestowed by the ascended Lord Jesus upon his church begin with the gift of the Spirit. As Peter said at Pentecost (Acts 2:33),

> Being therefore exalted at the right hand of God, and having received from the Father the promise of the Holy Spirit, he has poured out this which you see and hear.

Jesus lived a life of faith

So at every point the work of Jesus is the work of the Holy Spirit. All this leads to two very practical conclusions. The first is this: that if the characteristic work of the Spirit in human life is an experience of faith, an experience of God which ultimately has to be independent of our senses or feelings, then Jesus's life was above all a life of faith. He is, as Hebrews puts it, 'the pioneer and perfecter of our faith' (Heb.12:2). This really does make him one who was 'in all points tempted as we are' (Hebrews 4:15). It was not that he knew he was God in the same way as we know we are human beings – all we have to do is to look in a mirror. The only way he knew he was God was by the Spirit, that is, by faith. He knew he was God in the only way a Christian knows he is a Christian – by faith. We are not just saying here that we all have a life of faith, and Jesus was the best example of this. The truth is rather that his experience of faith was the source and standard of everyone else's before or since. The godly man's life of faith is only possible because Jesus pioneered the course himself.

Experiencing Jesus

The second point is this: that when we talk about the Spirit as the Spirit of Jesus Christ, we mean that all true experience of God must be at the same time an experience of Jesus. To be 'in the Spirit' means an experience of being 'in Christ'; to be 'led by the Spirit' means to experience the leading of the Lord Jesus Christ, and so on. It also means that no one can claim the authority of the Spirit to do something which does not correspond with the character of Jesus. People sometimes claim that the Spirit has led them to spend money which in fact was owing to someone else, to break promises, to engage in practices which were dubious, if not downright dishonest, or to neglect the needs of others, in the interests (supposedly) of the gospel. Such claims cannot be true.

But there are much deeper dimensions to the work of the Spirit of Christ in the New Testament. When the Bible talks about the work of the Spirit in a believer, it is not simply a matter of having an experience of God, but of being profoundly changed by the experience. This is the special concern of the epistles, but the gospels refer to it as well, especially the gospel of John.

The New Testament talks about the work of the Spirit as something that takes place deep in the spiritual make-up of those to whom he comes. The Spirit is with the followers of Jesus, and in them (John 14:16–17). Paul speaks joyfully of 'the love of God ... shed abroad in our hearts by the Holy Spirit which is given to us' (Romans 5:5). Speaking to the Corinthian Christians of the new life in Christ, Paul says, 'we are being changed into his likeness ...; this comes from the Lord who is the Spirit.' (2 Corinthians 3:18.)

New birth

This means that when we say that the Holy Spirit is God in our experience of Jesus Christ, we are not just talking about an experience which we might go through, think about, discuss, and perhaps dismiss into the past as a memory. At least, that is not the purpose of it.

The purpose of it is to change us. It is commonplace to say that the effect will be to make us more like Jesus; that is true, but the Bible is more definite than that. The chief ways in which the work of the Spirit is described are in terms of those great crises in the life of Jesus which we have been examining.

We saw that the first outburst of the Spirit's activities was at the birth of Jesus. Now, the beginning of the Christian life is likewise spoken of as a 'new birth'. People naturally turn to the famous chapter three of John's gospel for this; but practically every writer of the New Testament epistles refers to the new birth. Paul speaks of the 'laver of rebirth in the Holy Spirit' (Titus 3:5). James says that God gave birth to us of his own free will (James 1:18). Peter says we were born again of an incorruptible seed (1 Peter 1:23). But it is John who most clearly shows this to be the work of the Spirit. He records Jesus's words (John 3:6–8):

> Unless a man is born of water and the Spirit he cannot enter into the kingdom of God.... The wind blows wherever it wills ...; so it is with everyone that is born of the Spirit.

When Paul is writing to the Galatian Christians he insists that the only way to be a Christian is by faith, for that is the way of the Spirit. He feels that they have lost sight of this, and he is desperately upset about it. In his concern he uses an extraordinary phrase which expresses a similar idea. He says, 'I am in travail again until *Christ be formed in you*,' (Galatians 4:19). There is a wealth of insight into the meaning of the pastoral ministry there; but the immediate interest is the idea that in some sense when a person comes to know Jesus Christ a new life appears – the life of Jesus Christ himself. It is the background of the challenging little rhyme:

> Though Christ be born a thousand times anew
> Despair, O man, unless he's born in you.

This is a miracle. Just as miraculously as the Spirit came upon the girl Mary and God entered into the human race in the person of the man Jesus Christ, so he makes the life of that same Jesus begin and grow in the heart and life of anyone who puts their faith in him.

Baptism

The next great crisis was Christ's baptism. This is an obvious parallel, because baptism is recognized widely in Christian churches as the mark of entry into the Christian life. Now John the Baptist foretold Jesus as the one who would baptize, not in water, but in the Holy Spirit. Paul says that 'by one Spirit we were all baptized into one body' (1 Corinthians 12:13). Whatever else may be meant by baptism, it certainly means a new beginning; the entry into a new kind of life with new obligations and privileges. And just as when Jesus was baptized he began his ministry with a new endowment of the Spirit, so the Christian is 'born of water and the Spirit', and Peter proclaims the promise (Acts 2:38–39):

> be baptized in the name of the Lord Jesus and you will receive the gift of the Holy Spirit; for the promise is to you and to your children ... and to as many as the Lord our God shall call.

Christians disagree considerably, of course, as to the exact meaning of this connection between baptism and the Holy Spirit in practice. But there is no doubt about the fact that it is spoken of in Scripture.

A death

One of the most significant things is the way that Paul connects baptism with Christ's death. In Romans 6, with something of a tone of surprise, he says to his readers, 'What? don't you know that whoever is baptized into union with Christ Jesus is baptized into his death?' (Romans 6:3.) We shall be discussing the implications of this later on. But the important point to notice here is that there is a sense in which to become a Christian means to die. But we do not die *our* death; we die *his*. That is to say, if we are going to understand this mystery at all, we are not going to understand it by studying death as we know it in the world around us. We are not going to understand it by listening to people's theories about death.

A theological article on 'death' finely begins:

> From the biologist's point of view, death is no more than a phase in the rhythm of organic existence ... but it takes on a new significance when it is the death of the biologist himself. (Lovell Cocks, *A Handbook of Christian Theology*, page 76.)

For one thing we tend to regard death as a kind of annihilation. It is obviously not; it is more like the break-up of a set of relationships: between different parts of the body, between body and soul, between the person and people round about, and between the person and God. We are only going to understand this death as we look at the death of Christ, and as the Lord Jesus Christ makes it real to us by his Holy Spirit. What can be said briefly at this point is that Christ's death was meant to deal with sin; to pay its penalty, to break its grip over us, to make a free pardon morally justifiable and not a mere glossing over of sin. What happens is that this death for sin becomes real and effective in our lives by the Spirit. Paul says to the Corinthian Christians (1 Corinthians 6:11):

> You were cleansed, you were made holy, you were made right with God in the name of the Lord Jesus Christ, and in the Spirit of our God.

The simplest analogy of this is found in the Lord's Supper. When we eat food, the value of that food becomes effective in our bodies; it gives us energy and stamina. The kind of food we eat largely determines the sort of physical life we shall have.

Jesus Christ, by his Spirit, is the 'food' of our spiritual life. When we receive him, then what he is becomes effective in our character. And because he is above all One who has died for our sins, that fact determines the sort of spiritual life we shall have; it is one in which a death for sin has taken place. As a result, we can never regard sin in quite the same way again. It is no longer something we can tolerate as natural to life – it is an intolerable intrusion. Nor is it something, on the other hand, that we have to atone for, to make up for. That has been done already. God accepts us 'just as if we had never sinned'; but the fact that his death has somehow become a part of our lives means that we can never take that pardon for granted; repentance has been made a permanent part of our make-up. As he finished with sin on the cross, so in principle have we (Romans 6:10–11).

A resurrection

The Bible connects the Spirit with Christ's resurrection in a specially explicit way. And so for the Christian, 'If the Spirit of him who raised Jesus from the dead dwells in you, he ... will give life to your mortal bodies also through his Spirit,' (Romans 8:11). On the face of it, that looks like a promise that when we die, God will raise us to life again by the Spirit. But the context in Romans 8 suggests that Paul was thinking of a new life here and now. When he is writing to the Colossians, he apparently takes this for granted: 'If then you have been raised with Christ, seek the things that are above,' (Colossians 3:1). The Spirit is often spoken of as the source of life (John 6:63; Romans 8:2; 2 Corinthians 3:6; 1 Peter 3:18; Revelation 11:11). The life we live now by faith in Jesus is a 'risen' life. It is not completely 'risen' – the old dying creation hangs about us like old clothes that we are growing out of. But we have the first instalment of it ('the guarantee', Ephesians 1:14), a life which goes on for ever.

Again, it is vital to remember that this resurrection life is not to be imagined apart from Jesus Christ. Spiritists imagine a survival after death, and it is thought of as a refined version of this life. People think of living on, perhaps, in the lives of their children. Even Christians sometimes try to imagine life after death in material or abstract terms. Now we know that there are going to be some similarities with this life (Christ's resurrection body was not utterly unrecognizable, given the right conditions). But none of these methods of imagining what the 'risen life' is like are really Christian methods of doing it. What must be remembered is that we are 'alive in Christ'. While he is unseen, our life is unseen, too, 'hidden with Christ in God' (Colossians 3:3). And when he becomes physically visible, then so will our risen life as well (Colossians 3:4). And if we want to know what that risen life will be like, then the basic information we have is that 'we shall be like him' (1 John 3:2).

The pattern of continuing Christian experience

It now becomes clear that when the Spirit of Christ is at work in human experience the result is a sort of re-enactment, a 'reprint' of the birth, baptism, death and resurrection of Jesus in our make-up. Since these were single events in the past, it might be easy to get the impression that when a person becomes a Christian, he is born again, baptized into Christ Jesus, shares in his death for sin, and, being risen with Christ, now goes on plain sailing, so to speak.

This is not the whole story. Certainly birth and baptism are beginnings, and they can only really take place properly once (though in practice many people do seem sometimes to have 'false starts'). But they are beginnings, not the end of the matter. After birth comes growth, after baptism comes progress. And the growth and progress are patterned on the cross and resurrection. Paul speaks of his Christian service as 'dying daily' (1 Corinthians 15:31); he speaks of the need to 'reckon ourselves dead to sin' (Romans 6:11). He sees Christian life as working on the same principles as the cross; in dealing with sins in others he exhorts the Galatians to follow the principle of the cross – what he calls the 'law of Christ' – and bear one another's burdens of failure and shame (Galatians 6:1–2). He sees it in his own life as the principle upon which the power of the resurrection actually becomes effective. In pleading with the Corinthians to take notice of his letter, he goes on to say that his authority is like that of his Lord: like him, he comes to people vulnerable, capable of being crucified. And like him, by that very method he can draw from Christ the resurrection power of God (2 Corinthians 13:4).

This means that all through a Christian's life the Holy Spirit tends to take him through experiences patterned on that of the Saviour. He tends to be open to criticism and misunderstanding, even by friends, because he gets involved with people in trouble. Such people may well have brought it on themselves. And they may even let him down badly. He finds himself in opposition to vested interests and prejudices, in both worldly and religious people alike, in the cause of an honest and realistic service to God. He may find himself misrepresented and condemned by others, and unable to explain or defend himself. Where others can hide their self-interest or self-conceit behind a cloak of politeness, he finds his own exposed. Because of this, he is the more vulnerable because he cannot fight back on his own behalf; he cannot even enjoy the dubious comforts of a sense of heroism, for the cross continually makes him feel small. He cannot 'pull strings': if he is poor, people may despise him for his poverty. If he is rich, people may criticize him for self-indulgence. He cannot even begin to justify himself, because in trusting Christ, he has surrendered that question to God. In some societies, of course, the pattern may be worked out further, in arrest, trial, imprisonment and death. But whatever particular form it may take, the pattern of the cross is inevitable in a life 'in the Spirit'. As Jesus himself put it, 'Whoever does not bear his own cross and come after me, cannot be my disciple.' (Luke 14:27.)

At the same time, however, life also follows a resurrection-pattern. While some oppose us because the gospel challenges their interests, some key figure, a Roman soldier, or a Saul of Tarsus maybe, suddenly changes sides. While our sins are exposed, there is an ever-deepening sense of God's acceptance that holds us like an anchor in a storm, and life has that Easter morning freshness that only moral honesty makes possible. While people put us in the wrong and condemn us, and we cannot vindicate ourselves, someone in need meets us and in our presence has his own 'upper room' encounter with Christ. We, indeed, are not vindicated, but to those who need Christ, *he* is, and that is vindication enough. And the suffering church has both a history and a present-day story of martyrs through whom jailors and persecutors have been brought to faith in Christ.

Paul expressed things succinctly in a brief phrase to the Corinthian Christians who were causing him such heart-ache: 'So death is at work in us, but life in you.' (2 Corinthians 4:12.) And he goes on to speak of the Spirit of faith through which he has this confidence in the resurrection power of God. The Spirit of Christ does indeed tend to make Christians 'Christ-like'; but not through some programme of spiritual exercises or religious discipline (though this may have its place). The likeness is fashioned by taking the Christian along a path whereby he has to exercise the same kind of trust in God as Jesus did himself.

4

THE SPIRIT AND THE WORD

The Spirit of Christ: not just any notion of Christ, but as he is found in Scripture.

Readings: John 1:1–18; Genesis 1:26 – 2:7; Psalm 19; Ezekiel 2; Luke 24; 1 Peter 1:10–25; 2 Peter 1:16–21.

It is quite impossible to talk about the work of the Holy Spirit without noticing that in the Bible one of his outstanding activities was to inspire the prophets to speak from God. A prophet could even be identified in the Old Testament, not only as a man of God (1 Samuel 9:6; 1 Kings 13:29), but as 'he that has the Spirit' (Hosea 9:7). This affects more of Scripture than appears at first sight, because other people, beside the obvious ones in the Old Testament, were called 'prophets'. Abraham was a prophet and so was Moses (Genesis 20:7; Deuteronomy 34:10). In the Jewish grouping of Old Testament books, the books of Kings (for instance) were 'prophetic' books. Thus such writings were understood to be God's word – and words – to men (e.g. Joshua 1:5 in Hebrews 13:5).

The use of words for knowing God

There are some very important implications of this for the present day. Nowadays we are often oppressed by a feeling of the inadequacy of words. Many of the most passionate and profound experiences of life seem to be beyond words. From this arises the notion that words are inadequate to communicate the truth about God, and may be even positively misleading. The only way to know God, it is said, is by direct, personal encounter, which is really beyond words. All words can do is to 'witness' to it – suggest what we have seen. But we cannot give information, make true statements about him. This cuts at the root of the Bible's own conception of how God reveals himself to man by his Spirit. Among other things, it means that nothing that Jesus Christ himself could have said would tell us anything reliable about God!

To understand the issue here, I propose a brief digression. We need to realize what kind of being man is, and what he is doing when he uses words. And the first thing to note is that according to the Bible man is 'made out of the dust' (Genesis 2:7). That is to say, one aspect of his nature he shares with the rest of the material universe. Now a characteristic of matter, even in animal or vegetable form, is that it does not use words. Only man uses words. The psalmist, looking at the vast firmament above the world he lived in, exclaimed 'there is no speech, nor language,' (Psalm 19:3). And this wordless, material aspect of man's being is basic to his existence here. The instincts which enable us to survive physically as a race are wordless, and when we talk about them, we know that somehow our words do not create them; they only try to explain them. So it is true that man's basic experiences of life do not 'take kindly' to the use of words.

However, unlike the rest of the material creation, man is not merely of the dust. He is made in the image of God. God personally gave him a life from within the depths of his own being. This gave man a special place in creation, what the Bible calls 'dominion' (Genesis 1:26, Psalm 8:6). This has given man a special affinity with God and his way of doing things. Now one characteristic of God's mode of action which the Bible emphasizes is God's use of *words*. In the Genesis story the phrase appears repeatedly, 'and God said ...'. This is not just an accidental turn of phrase, because the psalmist makes a theme of it in Psalm 33:6 – 'by the word of the Lord were the heavens made'. The same teaching appears in Hebrews 11:3

– 'through faith we understand that the world was created by the word of God'. And Peter uses almost the same words (2 Peter 3:5). This does not mean, of course, that the Bible writers, or any one else, imagines that God created the world by talking in Hebrew across the void! But it does mean that man's ability to use words corresponds to a power in God's being whereby he has given creation the meaningful form which we know and appreciate. Man is made in God's image; and man's power to make and use words is patterned on something in the very nature of God.

So we must not underestimate the power of words. Much of man's inability to use words properly about God is attributed in Scripture not to the inadequacy of words, but to the fall of man into sin, falsehood and deceit. Jesus said, 'out of the abundance of the heart the mouth speaks,' (Matthew 12:34; Luke 6:45). When fallen man uses words, they are faulty and misleading because man's heart is faulty and deceptive (cf. Genesis 11:1–9). But the miracle is that 'God talks with man' (Deuteronomy 5:24), and when God uses words, then they speak truly about him. In point of fact, the idea that words are *necessarily* misleading with reference to God is derived from an outlook which belongs to religions like Buddhism and Hinduism rather than Christianity.

At the same time we must not attribute magical powers to words. Words are only symbols for the real thing; they can bring the reality to our minds and imaginations, but they do not of themselves involve us directly. This is their great value: it would be very inconvenient if, for instance, every time I said the word 'elephant', one appeared in my study! Certainly we can speak about God, and he may still hide his face from us. To think otherwise is a misunderstanding of the function of words which is very common indeed. For instance, it gives rise to the notion that theology is the same as spirituality; that if a person has the right words about God this makes him right with God. It can also give rise to superstitious anxieties in worship; the idea that without the right formula the worship is not accepted with God.

THE SPIRIT AND THE WORD

But these are misunderstandings. They give us no reason to reject the true value of words if we hear them from God himself. Words act like road signs enabling us to be sure that our route of thinking and action is sound; helping us to check on our experiences. Certainly some road signs in everyday life are faulty and let us down; but it would be silly to abandon their use altogether.

The spirit of our age does not, in general, regard words as much more than a clever device developed by man in the course of his supposed evolution. It is essential that we preserve the Bible's God-centred idea of words and their function. If we do not, we shall be constantly undermined by the feeling that the idea of God talking, or of finding out about God in a book, is a primitive and superstitious notion, not worthy of a truly 'spiritual' faith. The fact is that it is our use of words which enables us to look beyond the universe we live in. Without words, man could share no sense that life holds any meaning at all; indeed without words he could not even *deny* that it had any meaning!

The Spirit and the use of words

What we find then in the Bible is that although God's Spirit does work in creation without the use of words, he makes God's nature most clear to the creature made in his image through words. It is in verbal utterances that the Spirit does his most characteristic work. God speaks with man by the operation of his spirit. Man receives this in a form which can be expressed in words.

This occurs clearly in the Old Testament. Ezra prays to God and confesses: 'Thou gavest thy good Spirit to instruct them ... and didst warn them by thy Spirit through thy prophets.' (Nehemiah 9:20, 30.) In Isaiah 61:1–2 the prophet uses words which Christ claimed for himself: 'The Spirit of the Lord GOD is upon me, because the LORD has anointed me to bring good news to the afflicted.' It is impossible to imagine the Spirit giving instructions or good news without words. The prophecy of Ezekiel is punctuated by reference to the Spirit, and again, this is closely associated with God speaking to man (Ezekiel 2:2; 3:24). People listened to the prophet's words as being from God, carrying his authority; and on occasion these words were significant enough to be written down, so that others in later generations might read them as words uttered by the Spirit of God. So in Hebrews 3:7 a psalm is quoted as words which 'the Holy Spirit says'. 2 Peter 1:21 says of the prophets, 'men moved by the Holy Spirit spoke from God.'

There are even indications that, to a limited degree at least, a spirit claiming to be the Spirit of God could be tested by the words that were used. Thus, 'By this you know the Spirit of God: every spirit which confesses that Jesus Christ has come in the flesh is of God,' (1 John 4:2); 'no one speaking by the Spirit of God ever says "Jesus be cursed" ' (1 Corinthians 12:3). It is evident from the way in which the New Testament writers quote Old Testament texts that they were not concerned with the words in any magical way – trying to preserve the noises made when saying a sound, so to speak. They were concerned with words in respect of their meaning. And any words which did not correspond in meaning with scriptural statements about God would be rejected. It is that 'meaning' enshrined in the words which made the words so important to them as a test for truth.

So far, then, we can see that God makes himself known to man in Christ through his Spirit, and that man is given an understanding of who Jesus is by 'words which the Holy Spirit teaches' (1 Corinthians 2:13). (Much of this subject impinges on the doctrine of revelation and Scripture which is the subject of another book in this series. But such overlapping is to some extent inevitable: the truth about God is a unity, and we only divide it up for convenience in expounding it.)

Authority

This takes us a step further. The work of the Spirit in God's revelation produces words which have a special authority. There are true notions of God and therefore of Jesus Christ, and there are false ones, and these can be distinguished, in part at least, by using the 'words taught by the Holy Spirit'.

Election

This brings us to another characteristic of the Holy Spirit's work. The Spirit is selective in operation. This is most noticeable in the Old Testament. Repeatedly the Spirit came upon individuals 'out of the blue'. They were not necessarily obviously qualified. The Spirit came upon Gideon (Judges 6: 11–16, 34), a very insignificant candidate for national leadership. He came upon Balaam, a very unsatisfactory character for a prophet (Numbers 24:2). He came upon Saul, and this was so surprising that it became a proverb, 'Is Saul among the prophets too?' (1 Samuel 10:11–12). He made Amos – simple southern agricultural worker – a prophet to the corrupt and sophisticated court of the northern kingdom at Bethel. All the way through Scripture God selects and chooses people for specific tasks, privileges and destinies. This is dealt with in the biblical doctrine of election; and it has its equivalent in the way the Spirit works among men according to the Bible.

But in the New Testament this apparently goes by the board. When Peter quotes the prophet Joel at Pentecost as saying 'I will pour out my Spirit upon all flesh' it looks as if the day of selective activity is over. A closer look shows that this is not altogether the case. Peter expounds this and other prophecies by going on to say (Acts 2:38–39),

> Repent, and be baptized in the name of Jesus Christ, ... and you shall receive the gift of the Holy Spirit; for the promise is to you and your children, and to as many as the Lord our God shall call.

Now the offer of the Spirit of God is universal, but it was not indiscriminate. The Spirit is granted through Jesus Christ, and through him alone. And the only way in which the offer of the Spirit is universal is because the offer of Jesus Christ is universal. It is because Christ is offered for all men to receive that the Spirit is available. The two are bound up together: no Jesus, no Spirit. So Simon Magus in Acts 8:18–24 had not really come to terms with Jesus. This is shown by his attempt to buy the Holy Spirit, and the result is that the Spirit is not granted to him. The Spirit is still selective; his activity is restricted to Jesus Christ and his gospel, and only in relation to Jesus do people receive the gift of the Holy Spirit (see Romans 8:9–11).

The forming of the New Testament

As we shall see later in more detail, the 'gift of the Holy Spirit' is a very complex affair, involving a large number of different kinds of experience of God's grace. At the moment one particular aspect of it is of interest – the fact that in connection with the coming of Jesus the Spirit of God 'speaks' to man in a way that is parallel to the Old Testament. The result is a body of writings we call 'the New Testament'. To begin with, the work of Pentecost had a special meaning for the twelve, those first specially chosen disciples of Jesus. Acts 1:15 tells us that there were about 120 people in the upper room waiting for the Spirit, and apparently he came upon them all (Acts 2:1–4). But the eleven remaining after Judas's defection seem to have realized that they had a particular place in the infant church. They seem to have received rather more definite teaching than the others about the coming Holy Spirit, in John 20:19–28 (notice how Thomas is singled out for special treatment as 'one of the twelve', verse 24) and in Acts 1:8. These eleven felt it necessary to make up the number to twelve before the Spirit was bestowed on the church (Acts 1:15–26). This gave 'the twelve' a special authority when the Spirit came down; an authority of leadership in the church. Paul was subsequently added to that number, though he felt that he was hardly qualified for it. He confessed in 1 Corinthians 15:8–9 that he was about as qualified to bear the name as a baby that is born well after its time! Yet he also said that he was able to work effectively as an apostle by God's grace, and when challenged, he insisted upon his authority as an apostle on a par with the others (1 Corinthians 9:1–5).

Part of the work of the Spirit, then, was to create an apostolic circle of witnesses to Jesus Christ incarnate, crucified and risen. Their witness was to be an authoritative standard for whatever was to be taught in the church about Jesus. The authors of all four gospels were either apostles or their close associates. Paul himself claims to proclaim the gospel in 'words which the Holy Spirit teaches' (1 Corinthians 2:13; cf. 1 Corinthians 7:40 – 'I think I also have the Spirit of God'), and that his gospel is a criterion for any 'other gospel' (Galatians 1:6–9). Peter makes a similar claim to apostolic authority (1 Peter 5:12; 2 Peter 1:12–20). At the end of the second epistle Paul's letters are referred to as having an authority on a par with 'the other scriptures' (2 Peter 3:16). John makes a similar kind of claim for the book of Revelation (1:3; 22:18), and this is certainly connected if only in a general way with the work of the Spirit: he says (Revelation 1:10): 'I was in the Spirit on the Lord's day.' A similar kind of authority is claimed for John's gospel (John 21:24).

What it all adds up to is this. At Pentecost the Spirit of God came down on all those who belonged to Jesus Christ by faith. He inspired the believers to do many things, to perform miracles, prophesy, proclaim the gospel. He equipped a chosen group known generally as the twelve (e.g. Matthew 10:2; 1 Corinthians 15:5, and ten other references) and Paul (2 Corinthians 11:5; 12:11) to be the authority in the infant church about the truth concerning Jesus Christ. He inspired men to put that truth into writing within that circle of apostolic influence so that the authoritative teaching of the apostles would survive for every generation afterwards. To put it in a nutshell, he gave the apostles a special authority for the early church, and then brought the New Testament scriptures into being to exercise the same authority in the church after their death.

This means that the only conception of Jesus which can be certainly regarded as true is the one granted to us by the Scriptures. The language of these writings has come to us through the operation and selection of the Spirit. They speak to us of Christ, and no other kind of Christ is presented to our hearts by the Holy Spirit. It follows that any experience of God can only be accepted as the work of the Holy Spirit in so far as it presents to us Jesus Christ 'according to the scriptures' (1 Corinthians 15:3–4).

The search for reality

A consideration of our thinking about the Spirit's work up to this point will show that it corresponds with many of the difficulties that modern man has in seeking the meaning of life, or ultimate reality, or whatever he may like to call it. Certainly this age has been marked by a great search for reality through experience. The drug scene, the appeal of meditation techniques, the preoccupation with sex, the cultivation of a music with a volume that blots out the possibility of all reflection and critical thinking in direct experience – are all symptomatic. Much of the interest in charismatic experience is a christianized version of the same thing. The search is not an entirely futile one.

Intellectual and verbal activity is certainly not enough, and some spiritual experiences have been liberating and empowering. But others have been mixed blessings and still others have been utterly destructive. Now, in the experience brought about by the Spirit there is a decisive standard by which truth can be distinguished from error. But one of the characteristics of religious life in the past which has aroused a profound revulsion has been the tendency to define faith by formulas. One of the objections to putting teaching about God into verbal form has been that it seems to reduce the whole thing to something rigid and impersonal. The activity of the Spirit, however, is one which brings a man or woman into a very direct personal encounter with Jesus Christ as one with whom they have personal dealings and can enjoy a personal relationship. The words we use for doctrinal purposes have no power by themselves; their value is only that, by the Spirit, they indicate what he is like.

This longing for personal relationship is itself part of another search which could be summed up in a favourite word of the moment – 'involvement'. There is a profound sense that whatever constitutes 'real', 'authentic' living, it will require total involvement of the entire personality. Now, in practice people find it impossible to combine these demands. Mere experience, however stirring, does not lead to involvement. Indeed, it often causes people to 'drop out', to become uninvolved. And involvement which requires utter dedication to a cause or situation almost always leads to a situation in which one's critical faculties have to be suspended. The attitude of the critic is that of the spectator, not of the player; to be a critic one has to be detached, uninvolved.

But the Christian experience overcomes these conflicts. The Spirit who is the originator of our experience is the personal Spirit of Christ. Faith in Christ means that we become so involved with Christ that our very nature begins to undergo a change, by the same Spirit. This same Spirit has also brought into being his own description of the content and meaning of our experience. Scripture is the Spirit's own characterization of the person we are involved with. The involvement is so complete that even our reflective thinking is included in it, to be itself stimulated by the Spirit, as we consider and discuss just who it is we are dealing with. By a strange paradox, thinking *about* Jesus Christ as if we were just spectators discussing and analysing him becomes, by the Spirit, a fresh experience of *him*, closer to us than ever. The story of the disciples on the Emmaus road on the first Easter Sunday can be seen as a parable of this aspect of Christian experience. The Spirit makes it possible for us to converse, as it were, with the risen Lord Jesus as if he were absent (Luke 24:15–27)!

The Spirit applying Scripture

This brings us to another facet of the relationship between the Spirit and the Word of God. The Spirit is not only the one who has brought the Word into being; he is also at work in the receiving of it. In the Emmaus road story the disciples remarked, 'Did not our hearts burn within us ... as he opened up to us the scriptures?' (Luke 24:32.) It is by the Holy Spirit that Christ continues to do this in the hearts of those who belong to him. Jesus promised concerning the Spirit (John 16:14): 'He shall take what is mine and declare it to you.' This was at least to include Jesus's own words: 'He shall bring to your remembrance all that I have said to you.' (John 14:26.) In Hebrews 3:7 there is a remarkable expression which speaks volumes by its very casualness. The writer quotes from the Old Testament – from Psalm 95; and in the process writes, 'therefore, as the Holy Spirit says ...'. Not 'said', but 'says'. He finds, in this centuries old scripture, that the Spirit is actually saying it now! The same thing appears in Hebrews 10:15 – 'The Holy Spirit bears witness to us ...' followed by quotations from Jeremiah. The same idea, though without mention of the Spirit, appears in 2 Corinthians 6:2 – 'For he [God] says, "At the acceptable time I have listened to you ..."'. And this leads on to a mind-stopping punchline: 'the "acceptable time" is NOW!'

We can, with a little imagination perhaps, begin to see how it is that the New Testament is so saturated in references to the Old Testament. As they read it, the Holy Spirit was speaking to them of Christ: as they read it and thought upon it, the Holy Spirit brought them into living touch with Jesus. The way Peter saw it, the Spirit of Christ was in the Old Testament prophets pointing them to Christ, even though they themselves could not identify clearly just who it was they were talking about (1 Peter 1:10–11). Now although this work of the Spirit is only spoken of clearly in the New Testament with reference to the Old, there are hints that it was beginning to take effect with some New Testament writings as well. For instance there are unmistakable cross-references between Peter and Paul, between James and Matthew, and between Peter and Jude. (Romans 6:7 = 1 Peter 4:1; Matthew 5:34 = James 5:12; Jude 4–16 = 2 Peter 2:1–18.)

The interpretation of Scripture

This aspect, too, of the Spirit's work is still very strongly bound up with Jesus Christ. When Jesus said, 'You search the scriptures ... and they are they which testify of me' (John 5:39), he was laying down a basic principle: the scriptures can only be understood as first and foremost about Jesus Christ. It is in this respect that Scripture has its unique authority as God's word. It does, of course, provide a source of information about ancient history. We could learn a good deal about the geography and botany of the Holy Land from it. It is instructive about many other things as well. There is a great deal of vital teaching about morality; the Old Testament in particular offers some very striking insights into political and economic principles. There is in Scripture a whole philosophy of history, a profound understanding of man and his place in the universe, which is very important. But first and foremost, the Spirit speaks in Scripture about Jesus Christ.

It is not that the other subjects are not to be studied there. Actually in the New Testament reference is made to the Old Testament for a number of subjects – for example Paul goes to the Law of Sinai to show that gospel preachers have a right to be properly paid for their work, and he appeals to Genesis 3 for an argument about how women should behave in the church! But this use of the Scriptures is developed from a basic principle – that they are basically about Jesus Christ.

This is vitally important. The Spirit is the Spirit of Christ; the Spirit is the Author (from the divine point of view) of Scripture. And that means that the Scriptures are God's witness to Christ.

It might be helpful to see a few of the implications of this in practice. (To deal with it at length would involve us in the subject of hermeneutics, the science of biblical interpretation.) The fact is that the meaning of the language of any book is determined by its subject matter. For instance, we might take a phrase like 'labour unit'. If this were found in a book on industrial management, it would refer to the work that one man

could do in a given period of time. If the same phrase were
used in a book on hospital management, it would mean something vastly different! This is an extreme case that would only
raise a smile. But sometimes serious problems arise; for instance,
to a person talking theology, 'total depravity' means that in
every area of man's life, even at its best, something is 'off
course'. But to the ordinary man in the street it means complete
and utter degradation, and he reacts with violent annoyance to
such talk.

Now once we know what the subject of a communication is,
we know the kind of language we are dealing with, and we can
then make the right adjustments when we want to find out what
it says on a subject which is not its main concern. For example:
the Bible is not a book on astronomy, but it does talk about
the sun 'going down'. For the purposes of astronomy that would
be a very inaccurate statement about what happens to the sun
in the evening: but in terms of its subject-matter it is perfectly
satisfactory. If an astronomer wants to use such information for
his own purposes (e.g. in the case of Joshua 10:13 when the
'sun stayed still in the heavens'), he has to try to find out what
the words may mean in terms of his own subject first.

Neglect of this point very easily distorts the message of Scripture. It can be twisted into a blue-print for a political programme
(some 'revolution theology'), or a textbook on health (Christian
Science), or even for a heretical theory about God (Jehovah's
Witnesses). The Jews at the time of Jesus distorted it by making
the Old Testament a textbook on morality as a method of
earning God's favour. It blinded them to the true subject of
Scripture, Jesus Christ. As a result, even what the Bible does
say about morality – and theology – was hidden from them
(John 8:3–11; Matthew 22:29). So there is a principle that the
Spirit only speaks about any subject in Scripture in relation to
Jesus Christ; everything else has be understood in the light of
who he is and what he has done. (When you come to think of
it, that in itself must mean that Jesus Christ is God. For if the
Spirit is facing us with God, who else could so dominate his
message?)

The place of the Bible in our understanding of the Spirit's work means that we shall need to follow through some themes of Scripture in closer detail at this point. In this way we shall be able to see more clearly what actually happens when the Spirit comes into our lives and gets to work there.

5

THE FELLOWSHIP
OF THE SPIRIT

Not just individual experience, but experience in fellowship.

Readings: Matthew 18:15–35; 1 Corinthians 10–14; Galatians 5:16 – 6:10; Ephesians 4.

Quite recently in a discussion-time after an address, a lady asked me the meaning of a verse of Scripture. Before I could answer, she went on to give me her (quite reasonable) interpretation. Then she said that this interpretation had been given to her by the Spirit in answer to prayer. This was then offered as an argument that those who are led by the Spirit can receive their help from God without depending on human teachers.

Now I found my own reaction to this rather confused. In the first place, the interpretation she gave could have been found in a fair number of good commentaries, and I should have thought there was no lack of ministers who could have found these for her. Besides that, it was evident even to my limited scholarship that the text offered even more understanding of the Saviour than she had found in it, and it seemed that a miraculous work of the Holy Spirit should have done better than the commentators or myself. At the same time, I did not wish to be found criticizing the Holy Spirit! Other problems came thick and fast upon her conclusions. For instance, she was quoting the Authorized Version to me, and it was obvious therefore that she was not making her own translation. So she was certainly depending very heavily on human teachers at that point at least. Furthermore, if she was so independent of human teachers, why had she come to listen to me? Admittedly something in her tone of voice did suggest that perhaps she was actually there to teach me rather than to be taught; and I could appreciate this, since most teachers will admit that they learn prodigiously from those they are supposed to teach. But if I were to accept her conclusions, then clearly I too would not need her teaching anyway!

Now this kind of thinking is not uncommon. There is enough support in Scripture to show that there must be a certain truth in it (Psalm 119:99; 1 John 2:27), but obviously something has gone wrong somewhere. The fact is that there is no conceivable way in which we can find Christ in the Scriptures without the help of other Christians. Without nineteen hundred years of Christians hiding, preserving, translating, publishing and distributing Scripture, we would not even have a Bible. This is means whereby it comes to us. In other words, the Holy Spirit brings God's word to us through his people, the church. This, in fact, is the normal way in which he makes Christ known to mankind, and it needs some careful consideration.

What is the church?

Many people react uncomfortably to mention of the church, because the word conjures up in their minds certain ideas. And these ideas seem to have very little to do with the rich, joyous simplicity of Christian life as it is found in the New Testament. There are thoughts of business meetings, of organization, of lofty cathedrals, and rather remote clerical leaders. Stories come to mind of ordinary people forgotten or even ill-treated by church leaders. The personal touch seems to be all too easily lost.

Actually, the New Testament conception of Christian life is not quite as simple and unorganized as we are tempted to think. The local churches, for instance, always had people with some official status (Acts 6:1–6; 14:23; Titus 1:5) who had a recognizable authority (Acts 15:22, 20:28; Hebrews 13:7; 17, 24). There were rules, and there could be formal excommunication (2 Thessalonians 3:10, 14; 1 Corinthians 5:4–5). The worship was not entirely informal, since there are evidences of what we could call 'set prayers' – the Lord's Prayer is an obvious example. Worship was apparently modelled on that in the synagogues. James even speaks of the church as a 'synagogue' (James 2:2; Greek)! Charitable funds were organized and distributed (Acts 11:29; 1 Corinthians 16:1–3), and even then some got neglected (Acts 6:1). There was the danger that leaders could seek money or power through their position (1 Peter 5:2; 3 John 9). But at the same time, there is no indication that such circumstances were ever regarded as the essence of the church. They were inevitable in the proper functioning of the church, but the church itself was the people. The organization has been likened to the mechanism of a piano; the music is always to some extent marred by the sound of it, but nevertheless, it makes the music possible. Perhaps our complaint about church organization should be not that its existence cramps our freedom, but that it is often too obtrusive. Put another way, the church is like the individual Christian; accepted by God as righteous, even though in practice he falls short. God sees the church as the fellowship of all those who are indwelt by the Spirit of Christ; we see it as a very faulty institution. But if the Spirit of God is prepared to dwell in it and work with it, so must we.

The church as the Spirit's work

In Matthew 16:18 Christ said, 'I will build my church,' and he did that by the Holy Spirit. In Acts 2 the Spirit came upon the disciples and they became an apostolic fellowship to which other people became attached (verses 41–42). Those who were baptized in the name of Jesus Christ became members of that body 'by one Spirit' (1 Corinthians 12:13). In Ephesians 4:13, the unity of that body is the work of the Spirit, and discord is a challenge to him (compare Ephesians 4:29–32 and Romans 14:13–19). Paul's closing benediction in his second letter to the Corinthian church torn by party divisions includes a prayer for the 'fellowship of', or 'common participation in' the Holy Spirit. The nature of that fellowship is spelled out for us in 1 John 1:3–7 – 'that you may also have fellowship with us, and indeed our fellowship is with the Father and with his Son Jesus Christ.'

This fellowship is not only created by the Spirit, but it can be maintained only by him. In Acts 4 when the infant church finds itself under attack, an appeal is made to God for help. The result is a renewed outpouring of the Spirit and a fresh cementing of the bonds of faith: 'Now the company of those who believed were of one heart and one soul....' (Acts 4:32.) This expressed itself outwardly in a voluntary commitment of personal possessions into a common pool, so that poverty, for the time being at least, was overcome. When Ananias and Sapphira pretended to share in this, Peter said that they were lying, not against him or the church, but 'against the Holy Spirit' (Acts 5:3). It was not keeping part of the money that was wrong. It was their dishonesty that challenged the whole atmosphere of mutual trust.

The church indwelt by the Spirit

In Ephesians 2:20–22, there is a surprisingly comprehensive description of the church. The church is like a building, says Paul; the foundation-layer is the apostles and prophets. The whole edifice is built round and on Christ, the cornerstone, without whom the entire structure would collapse. It is a temple in which God might have his abiding presence. This presence would be realized by God's Spirit. To paraphrase that in terms of what we have been saying up to now: the church is to be a community in which God is to be met with by faith in the Lord Jesus Christ.

A temple, of course, was a place of worship; and this too is the work of the Spirit. Jesus said to the woman of Samaria, 'God is Spirit, and those who worship him must worship in spirit and in truth.' (John 4:24.) Paul says of Christians, they 'worship God in spirit ...' (Philippians 3:3). There is an alternative phrase in some ancient manuscripts – 'worship by

the Spirit of God' (RSV margin). We may not be sure which
is the original; but this second form shows how the early church
understood the meaning of Paul's words. He meant that true
worship of God was only offered when our spirit worships him
through the power of the Holy Spirit. Paul's exhortation on
how Christians ought to conduct their worship in 1 Corinthians
12 and 14 is fraught with references to the Holy Spirit. It is
he who gives gifts that make the worship possible.

In 1 Corinthians 12:12–26 Paul uses one of his favourite metaphors for the church – a body. The Spirit indwells the church
like life in a body, strengthening, directing and correcting it.
Examples of this are especially found in Acts. In Acts 9:31 after
the conversion of Paul, the continuing growth and confidence
of the church was 'in the comfort of the Holy Spirit'. In Acts
13:1–4 the Spirit chose and sent out Paul and Barnabas as missionaries. It is not clear in detail how this took place (perhaps
it was on the lines of Acts 11:27–30), but it certainly happened
in a general atmosphere of worship and prayer in the church
gathered together for that purpose. When the church had to
face its first great crisis of doctrine and practice – the inclusion
of non-Jews – there was considerable discussion. But eventually
a decision was reached. In the letter recording this, the
Jerusalem church was so conscious of the presence of God by
his Spirit that they wrote, 'It has seemed good to the Holy Spirit
and to us ...' (Acts 15:28).

This presence of the Holy Spirit in the church is referred
to in the book of Revelation in a remarkable way. In the first
three chapters various churches are addressed and rebuked or
encouraged by letters. The beginning of each letter speaks of
its words as those of the exalted Lord Jesus whom John had
seen in a vision (Revelation 1:12–20). The end of each letter
says of the same words 'hear what the *Spirit* says to the
churches'. What he is implying is that what the Spirit does and
says is what Christ does and says. We are back to the fact that
the Spirit's work is to make the unseen Lord of the universe
a reality independent of our sense-experience.

There seem to be two senses at least in which we can understand this. The first sense comes from these letters in Revelation and from Ephesians 2:22. Here the idea is that the Spirit is at work making Christ a reality in the ongoing life of the church, strengthening, directing and correcting it. It is a long-term process in which the Lord builds up understandings of his truth and preserves his gospel over years and even centuries, through all the ups and downs of church life, either local or universal.

The second sense is more immediate. Jesus said, 'Where two or three are gathered together in my name, there am I in the midst,' (Matthew 18:20), and this is with reference to decisions which might have to be made in a small fellowship. This situation is much more like the sort of situations we have been looking at in Acts 4, 9 and 13. Here the Spirit is at work giving individual Christians, and groups of Christians, specific guidance as to what to do next. It is an experience which is, in the nature of the case, much more vivid and easy to identify than that of the experience of the church across the centuries and generations of its history. But they are not completely separated; in fact, in the case of Acts 15, the 'council of Jerusalem' embraces both. The local experiences all feed into the larger ones. Not only so, but the larger ones feed back into the local situations. We can see that from the fact that the life of the church at Antioch in Acts 15:30, and the guidance of the Spirit to Paul and Silas in the next chapter, are all based on the major policy decision made at Jerusalem (Acts 15:22 onwards).

All this means that the indwelling of the Spirit in the church is not confined to some general guidance of its history, nor only truly found in the experiences in local groups of gathered Christians, but includes both. A tragic example of this truth can be found in the history of Pentecostal movements of the last 150 years. The miraculous power and freedom of the Spirit which the early Pentecostals stood for did not fit easily into the doctrinal and organizational forms of the historical church. Unhappily a separation took place. The result was that for a century or more the main body of Christian church life was deprived of a whole dimension of experience of the Spirit, and at the same time, the Pentecostals themselves became cut off from the vital theological tradition whereby God's work could be properly understood and assessed. The result was that the presentation of what they knew, and the argument for it, were pathetically weak. Indeed, it is only recently that the level of debate on subjects like the baptism of the Spirit and the gift of tongues has been worth much more than the paper it was written on. Very often the aspect of the Spirit's work in the church which is hardest to accept is the very aspect we most need for our fuller vision of Jesus Christ. We hardly scratch the surface of the breath-taking range of his potential among us.

The gifts of the Spirit [See also Appendix 2]

Once again we find the Spirit and Jesus Christ almost identified in Ephesians 4:7. The grace which every Christian enjoys is spoken of as Christ's gift, the outcome of his ascension into heaven. But following that there is a reference to gifts for the church as well as the individual – apostles, prophets, evangelists, pastors, teachers. In 1 Corinthians 12:28 the list is somewhat different – apostles, prophets, teachers, miracle-workers, healers, helpers, administrators, speakers in tongues. Obviously neither is meant to be exhaustive. Now earlier in 1 Corinthians 12 there is another list (verses 8–10), with very similar items: utterances of wisdom, knowledge, faith, gifts of healing, working miracles, prophecy, the discernment of spirits, tongues, and interpretation. In this case they are spoken of as 'gifts', and they are 'energized' and allotted by the Spirit 'as he chooses' (verse 11), and they are 'manifestations of the Spirit' (12:7; 14:12). They are called 'spiritual gifts', and some of them at least were called 'spirits' – perhaps for short (12:1, 14:1, 14:32).

There is plenty of material for discussion and controversy here! We shall try to keep for the most part to some main lines of thought.

The first point of interest is that there are certain differences between the lists. The Ephesians 4 list says that the gifts of Christ are *people*. They are people who have what might be called official, or semi-official functions. We can see this more clearly when we compare it with the second list in 1 Corinthians 12:28. It would be difficult to appoint a person to the office of miracle-worker, and almost impossible to appoint a 'helper'! In both cases the activity is too vague. So it looks as if here we are thinking about the church as a society of believers headed up by the risen Lord himself who appoints those who have leadership in the church. Elsewhere in the New Testament there are indications of how the people with official responsibility in the early church were appointed. The normal practice was by 'laying on hands' (Acts 6:6; 13:3; 1 Timothy 4:14; 5:22; 2 Timothy 1:6). The same act was used in other situations for healing the sick (Mark 16:18) and for giving the empowering gift of the Holy Spirit to believers (Acts 8:17–18, 19:6).

In two cases where this phrase is used of an appointment (1 Timothy 4:14; 5:22), some other interesting facts emerge. In both cases there is reference to a 'gift' received on the occasion. Not only that but in the first one there is also a reference to prophecy, another of the gifts referred to in the lists in 1 Corinthians 12; and in the second there is an immediate allusion to the sort of 'Spirit' given – not of timidity, but of power, love, and self-control. It seems pretty clear that normally when a person received the laying on of hands in this manner, he also received some kind of experience of God's power. We may understand from no less an example than Jesus himself that it was not automatic (Mark 8:23), but it seems to have been expected, at least. In the case of Timothy, it would be a gift which would equip for his office. We can draw a general and perhaps tentative conclusion that when Christ gave the gifts of leadership to his church, along with their appointment the Spirit would bestow gifts which would enable them to do their work effectively.

The second list in 1 Corinthians 12:28 is also of people. But here the list is not just about leadership. Certainly God is said to 'appoint' them, but the word here simply means 'to set in its place'. This follows from the argument of the previous verses about the various parts of the body. It seems to mean that God has determined what part each shall play in the life of the body.

This is supported by the way the chapter ends by talking about the use of gifts. The people in this list have a place in the church which depends on the kind of gifts they possess, whether common or remarkable.

The third list, in 1 Corinthians 12:8–10, is not of people, but of powers. These enable people to do certain special things. And the mystical number nine in the list may be a hint that this is meant to be comprehensive.

There has, of course, been a great deal of discussion about the items in this list, but one thing is fairly clear, that these gifts were all in a special sense supernatural. This is indicated by the fact that they are all called 'spiritual'; and the reasoning in chapter 14 comparing prophecy with glossolalia (speaking in tongues) is obviously meant to have some reference to the whole list.

Of course there is a sense in which the whole Christian life is supernatural. But there are degrees of 'supernatural-ness'. Some experiences, even among Christians, were supernatural enough to be called 'miracles'; and some of these could even be called 'extraordinary miracles' (Acts 19:11). In this list, miracles are only one item; nowadays we would have probably included spiritual healing under that heading, but Paul and the Corinthians evidently did not. One gets the impression that their whole understanding of miracles was more sophisticated than ours.

Probably the best way to understand this list would be to start with the ones about which we have some definite information.

In 1 Corinthians 14, Paul refers to prophesying as similar in nature to speaking in and interpreting tongues. In verse 14, he describes what happens as 'my spirit praying'. Later on, in referring to prophecy, he speaks of 'the spirits of the prophets' (verse 32). So these gifts involve an activity of a person's 'spirit'. In the case of tongues verse 14 says, 'my mind is unfruitful,' that is, it does not make any contribution. What takes place then is an ecstatic utterance in which the conscious mind does not supply the content, as happens in normal speech. If the utterance is in a strange tongue, then obviously the speaker cannot understand it without interpretation. But it would also be possible for a quite intelligible ecstatic utterance to take place in which the conscious mind still does not control what is being said. In which case it could be a 'word of prophecy', or of 'wisdom', or 'knowledge'; something which could be termed 'a revelation' (verse 6). What happens is that the Spirit of God energizes the personality of the speaker, but in so doing by-passes his normal powers of choosing what he wants to say and how to say it.

All this may sound a bit eerie and spiritistic to those who are not used to it. In a sense it is. But there are certain essential differences. The first is that the Spirit who gives these gifts and powers is the Spirit of Christ. This has already been laid down at the beginning of chapter 12. In spiritism (or spiritualism, as it is often called) a medium seeks to empty the mind, and allow spirits to make contact. Paul is talking about something quite different when he says, 'I speak in tongues more than you all,' (1 Corinthians 14:18); here he is seeking to fill his mind and heart with the glory of Jesus Christ.

Secondly, the Spirit does not take away the power of control. An ecstatic speaker cannot decide what to say, but he can decide whether to say it and when to stop. 2 Timothy 1:7 says the Spirit is the Spirit of self-control; again, the spirits of the prophets are subject to the prophets. In the case of spiritism the spirits increasingly 'take over' the person involved. This is why Paul has no hesitation in calling for an ordered use of such gifts (1 Corinthians 14:27–28, 40); no one can plead, 'I couldn't help it.' Indeed the Spirit actually develops our self-control.

Thirdly, the results of such utterances are always subject to test (1 John 4:1). They do not carry an absolute authority. The spirits can always be called upon in the name of the Lord Jesus to identify themselves. Spirits which refuse to be put to the test (they often suggest that to do this would be unbelief and sin), or which give no opportunity for such testing, are not of God. Such testing relates, firstly, to what the spirits teach or say they believe – that Jesus Christ is Lord (1 Corinthians 12:3) and that he became truly man (1 John 4:2–3); and secondly by their conformity to Scripture and its doctrines. Even an angel from heaven must not preach any gospel but salvation by grace through faith (Galatians 1:8)! And no spirit can command some-one to act contrary to Scripture. Then there is a long term test for prophecy – it is false if it does not come to pass. Finally, the gifts of the Spirit are not really for our own personal satisfaction alone; they are above all intended for building up the body of Christ, however much individuals may benefit (Ephesians 3:18; 4:12; 1 Corinthians 14:4–5).

The gifts of utterance – wisdom, knowledge, prophecy, tongues and interpretation – are all of this order. There are principles at work in these gifts which make it easier to under-stand the others. In speaking in tongues, the Spirit by-passes the mental process of choosing words to say. In healing and miracles, the power of the Spirit by-passes the normal physical processes whereby we usually control or affect the natural course of events, introducing new chain reactions of cause and effect. In the gift of faith – the power to trust God for extraordinary events to happen (cf. 1 Corinthians 13:2) – and the discernment of spirits, the power of the Spirit by-passes the normal limitations of reasoning about causes, effects, symptoms, and introduces some intuitive conviction about the spiritual truth of a situation. It must be remembered that these are gifts, not God, although God's spirit is the energy exercised in them. This means that they can be abused, and sometimes a right use of them can be combined with mixed motives, and degrees of ignorance, weak-ness and even error. It is plain that even in Corinth, where people were much more used to this kind of thing than we are, the whole matter called for considerable godly wisdom and common sense. But there are indications that where spiritism is widespread (such as in witchcraft or occultism), these gifts may well be needed. (For treatment of individual gifts, see Appendix II).

The Spirit and the sacraments

The reference to the fact that the gift, or gifts of the Spirit frequently accompanied the laying on of hands in the New Testament raises some further questions. What is the connection between such an act and the experience that went with it? The laying on of hands was not the only symbolic act in the New Testament church. There were two others which had even greater significance because they are connected with our Lord's own commands to his apostles. These are, of course, baptism and the Lord's supper, often called 'ordinances' because they were ordained by Christ's own words. From time to time other acts have had some similar significance in the church's life. The difficulty in understanding what happens in such rites is simply this: the gospel insists that the grace of God is in no way tied to *any* human action such that just doing the act would obtain the grace, and the church's experience supports this. But the Scriptures speak of a connection between the sacraments and the work of the Spirit so close that the principle almost seems to be contradicted. And Christians have never been able to do without sacramental rites of some sort (on baptism: Romans 6:3–4, 1 Peter 3:21; on the Lord's Supper: 1 Corinthians 10:21; 11:23–29). There have been many more or less satisfactory explanations in the church's history.

Some at least of these problems disappear when we consider them in the light of the doctrine of the Holy Spirit. To begin with, whatever 'grace' or 'gift' is associated with the sacraments, it must be the work of the Holy Spirit. Now the Spirit's characteristic work is to arouse a faith-awareness of Jesus Christ's presence. Our understanding of Jesus is brought to us through the Scriptures, that is through words. Now words are symbols; and they are not the only symbols we use. For instance the word STOP could equally be represented by a red light, or the raised hand of a policeman. Actions like baptism and the breaking of bread are acted symbols of the gospels: they can function in the same way as Scripture, as God speaking to us, especially since they are appointed in Scripture.

But acted symbols work in a very interesting way. A simple example could be a handshake. It is a symbol of friendship. If I offer to shake hands after a quarrel, it is an appeal for reconciliation. And we see sacraments work in this way. On the one hand they are God's acted invitation to us; his word in symbol

form. When we know what they mean, and we intend to respond
to God's invitation, and we are physically capable of doing so,
then they are our way of saying 'Yes' to God, and something
actually happens, just as much as something happens when we
put our signature to a contract, or shake hands on a bargain.
These actions are the normal way of 'signing the contract'. There
are often many other ways, and they may be necessary when the
usual way has become misunderstood or abused. But they are
still the normal way, because that is the way the Lord ordained
them. So baptism is for that once-for-all commitment of the new
birth, and the Lord's Supper is for the repeated renewal of it
in all the changing scenes of life, as the world, the flesh and the
devil challenge us as to the sincerity of that commitment. (This
understanding of the sacraments has no bearing one way or
another on the debate concerning infant baptism. The nature
of an infant's faith as bound up with that of his parents and
sponsors, and the nature of church membership, are separate
issues outside the scope of this book.)

If the other person understands my action, wants to make it
up, and shakes my hand, that actually clinches it. Something
definite takes place through the action; the attitudes are no longer
'just in the mind', something which could be questioned quite
easily by others. Others might *see* the handshake; it becomes part
of ordinary experience, ordinary history, as it were. If the other
person refused to shake hands, then the reconciliation would not
take place. So to some extent, shaking hands can reconcile
people, and not shaking hands can keep them apart.

But there are very important conditions controlling the way
this works. It depends on whether the people concerned can
physically perform the action. It would be ridiculous to think
that a person with no arms could not make up a quarrel because
he could not shake hands! Baptism and Holy Communion likewise are not the *only* means whereby their purposes can be
fulfilled in Christian life. Again, we recognize that if someone
from some other culture had been brought up to think of an
outstretched hand, as meaning, say, a demand for money, then
the thing would not work. Both parties have to understand what

the action means. Similarly, there are sometimes serious distortions of the meaning of the sacraments. They become symbols of a general assent to a church's social life, or some such vague notion. Finally, we recognize that the intention behind the act has to be appropriate. There are cases where this is not so. For instance, a kiss is a symbolic expression of affection. But Judas betrayed the Son of Man with a kiss. In such a case, the act does not 'do' what it is intended to do. If it is done deceitfully or meaninglessly or off-handedly then it still *does* something – it produces an opposite effect. A false reconciliation will end up with a more intractable quarrel than ever. So Paul says that a person who eats and drinks the communion elements 'in an unworthy manner' drinks damnation to himself; it would be like wiping one's feet on a national flag in the presence of that nation's leader.

But there is a further dimension to the sacraments. They are not solitary individual actions; they are church acts. They are done by at least 'two or three gathered' in the name of Jesus. They are expressions of the fellowship of the Spirit. We are baptized into one body; the bread we break is a participation in the body of Christ, and we are 'one loaf' (1 Corinthians 10:17). So in the sacraments the Word of Christ, the personal commitment of faith and the fellowship of God's people are all brought together as a situation in which the Spirit may make God especially real to our hearts in Jesus Christ.

Christians can no more exist spiritually without the church than they can exist without a natural family. But we could still ask the question, what is the church for? What is the purpose of such an arrangement?

6

THE SPIRIT
OF PROCLAMATION

The Spirit does not just keep the church going; he keeps it going out into the world with the gospel.

Readings: Psalm 100; Isaiah 66:17–24; Acts 1 and 2; 1 Corinthians 1:7–2:16.

When Jesus gave his final promise to the first disciples in Acts 1:8 he did it to correct a misunderstanding. They had asked him whether this was the time for their own nation to rule the world; and of course this implied that they would have important positions in the new age. His reply was virtually to tell them to mind their own business. The Holy Spirit would come upon them, not to exalt them, or even consolidate the movement Jesus had started, but rather to scatter them all over the world with the power to bear testimony to Christ. Ever since then the church has kept trying to consolidate itself, to build an empire, to secure its own niche in society. And repeatedly when it has settled down too much it has lost its power to speak effectively for Christ. And just as repeatedly the Spirit has shaken it up and sent its best men out into the world at large.

The process can be detected very early on in the story. Events following Pentecost produced a rapid growth of the church. Preaching and teaching went on apace, and even many priests were converted (Acts 6:1, 4–5). Then the work of the Spirit through Stephen's outspokenness rocked the boat badly, and persecution resulted (Acts 6:10; 7:51, 55–58; 8:1). The church was scattered throughout Judea and Samaria, leaving only the apostolic nucleus behind. Back to square one! From the point of view of the authorities, it was the worst thing they could have done. Like sycamore seeds on the wind, the Christians took the gospel with them wherever they went, and new churches began to take root and grow (Acts 8:4). The chapters following speak of Christians in many villages in Samaria and at least one town there (8:5, 25); in Damascus (9:1–2) in the north, Caesarea (9:30), Lydda (9:32), and Joppa (9:36) on the coast. And these are clearly but a few of many (9:31). Saul's furious attempts to suppress the new sect begin to look like a man trying to catch feathers in a gale. The Christians went further still; outside the Holy Land altogether, north to Phoenicia and beyond, to Antioch; across the sea to Cyprus (11:19). Everywhere they went they told their fellow Jews about Christ.

But this was not the worst of it. After all, Jews were found everywhere in the eastern Mediterranean, and they were a fairly close community; they stood by one another in a world from which their Law kept them segregated. There had, after all, been other Messiah-sects in Judaism that had their appeal. But the Spirit got to work again. He arranged a preaching engagement for Peter before a completely non-Jewish congregation, and then interrupted the sermon with a mini-Pentecost! They had not even applied for circumcision! Peter bowed to the facts and baptized them, Gentiles though they were, as Christians (Acts 10). Actually similar 'irregularities' were also happening elsewhere (11:20–21) and the Holy Spirit encouraged it, through Barnabas (Acts 11:22–24). Eventually the church had to face the fact that their vision was being enlarged; that when Jesus had said 'make disciples of all nations', he had not meant 'make disciples of Jews in all nations'. He had meant it literally....

Mission in the Old Testament

Christians often think of 'mission' as something which started in the New Testament. This in a sense is true, but it was an extension of Old Testament ideas. It is easy to overlook the fact that although the Old Testament was formed among the Jews, its history goes back to Adam, and the first promise of a Saviour for man was given to the descendants of Eve, not to a Jew. God was showing favour to men before there was such a thing as a Jew. Nor is the story that followed particularly complimentary to the Jewish origins. Even Abraham has to accept the rebuke of a heathen king (twice – Genesis 12:18; 20:9). Jacob was a dubious character by any reckoning; the ancestors of the twelve tribes (except for Joseph) show up badly. Joseph is indeed their rescuer; but not before he had first become the rescuer of the Egyptians. The spiritual history of the Jews shows a Gentile interest. The promise to Abraham for Isaac was that 'in your seed shall *all the nations* of the earth call down a blessing on themselves' (Genesis 12:1–3). So the judgements on Egypt were that 'my name might be declared throughout all the earth' (Exodus 9:16).

At significant points one finds that non-Jews came into privileged positions. Ruth the Moabitess was the ancestor of King David. Rahab the Canaanite (a people under an interdict) came into Israel, and in the next chapter Achan, a blue-blooded Judahite, was condemned and destroyed. In the golden glow of the age of Solomon, the Queen of Sheba comes to acknowledge the God of Israel. Almost every prophet has some message for the non-Jewish nations. They were not very encouraging, it is true, but their judgements were no worse than those upon the people of Israel, and they are often accorded real respect, even sympathy, and sometimes hope (Ezekiel 26–28; Jeremiah 49:6, 39; Isaiah 19:24–25). In one case there is a prophet who virtually goes through the same sort of challenge that Peter went through with Cornelius. Jonah had to face the fact that God cared about the heathen city of Nineveh enough to pardon it. And Nineveh was the capital of the most brutal oppressor Old Testament Israel ever had to endure. Isaiah's prophecy ends with a vision of missionaries declaring the Lord's glory among all the nations (Isaiah 66:19). And constantly in the temple and synagogues the Psalms would lead the nation's praise to a God who was to be known and praised throughout the world (Psalm 2:10; 18:49; 46:10; 47:1; and references in about twenty other psalms).

The limitation of the Old Testament vision was that it necessarily dealt with symbols. The nation of Israel was, among other things, the symbol for God's presence with mankind, representing him in a provisional kind of way. She represented Christ who was to be born Emmanuel, 'God with us'. He was to be a 'light to lighten the Gentiles, and the glory of thy people Israel' (Luke 2:32). The fact is that Israel was nothing without him; he *was* Israel, in fact.

The truth of this emerges when we compare some New Testament passages about Jesus Christ with the Old Testament. In John 15:1 he calls himself the real vine, in comparison and contrast with Israel in passages like Isaiah 5:1–7; Jeremiah 2:21; Ezekiel 15:2. In the Old Testament, virtually the only way to find God was to come to Israel. In Israel, in symbols and types, it was possible to meet with the God who later showed himself as the God and Father of our Lord Jesus Christ. When Jesus came, he offered himself as all that the Jewish nation had ever been created for. When the Jews rejected him, the only interpretation left to them of the old prophecies was a literal, self-centred, nationalistic one.

The New Testament

Once the early Christians had been taught the Spirit's lesson, that all nations were to come to Christ, the call to proclaim the gospel was 'let loose'. Paul was the outstanding exponent of this. In Ephesians (3:6) he says that he was vouchsafed a special insight into this phase of human history –

> how the Gentiles are fellow heirs, members of the same body, and partakers of the promise in Christ Jesus through the gospel.

In this way what began as a rather uncertain obedience by some, and an irregular enthusiasm by others, became the church's life-style – 'the work of the ministry' (Ephesians 4:12). They 'sounded forth' the gospel as by a trumpet throughout the Greek peninsula (1 Thessalonians 1:8). Domestic life became a mission-field (1 Corinthians 7:16; 1 Peter 3:1). Daily life as a citizen was a sphere in which to win glory for God (1 Peter 2:12–15). Even as church-centred an act of worship as the breaking of bread was to 'proclaim' the Lord's death; and it was expected that when Christians met for worship others might come in and become confronted with the presence of God (1 Corinthians 11:26; 14:21–25). In this way, 'Jews or Greeks, slaves or free – all were made to drink of one Spirit' (1 Corinthians 12:13). Every possible restriction was broken down to a degree we still find difficult to cope with; the Spirit sowed the word in every social class, every culture, every language group, profession, territory, colour. He then insisted that those who became Christians should accept each other *as they were*, and then go on to look for others.

The Spirit and preaching

The spokesmen for the gospel in the New Testament all reckoned to preach 'in the power of the Spirit' (Luke 24:49; 1 Thessalonians 1:5). Luke indicates that Jesus himself preached in the power of the Spirit (Luke 4:14–19), and in the parallel in Mark 1:22, there is a stress on the authority of his preaching, which could be a reflection of this. It is evident that when the Spirit fell upon the disciples at Pentecost. almost immediately there was an urge to preach. Paul, referring to his own preaching to the Corinthians, wrote (1 Corinthians 2:4–5):

> My speech and my message were not in plausible words of wisdom, but in demonstration of the Spirit and power, that your faith might not rest in the wisdom of men but in the power of God.

This emphasis on preaching calls for further comment.

In the first place, a study of Acts shows that preaching was not quite the sort of thing that we take for granted today. Although formal preaching in the synagogues did take place, it was only a small part of apostolic preaching. They had comparatively few requests to deliver carefully rounded 25-minute (or 10-minute) addresses. Most of their preaching was more direct communication with the hearers, and it was delivered anywhere where people could be persuaded to listen. It was often in the open air; but it is doubtful whether the apostles would have bothered to compete with the noise of traffic and the constant surge of pedestrians in the way that open-air preaching sometimes does today. Preaching simply meant announcing the good news whenever and wherever there was an opportunity to get people to listen. So we can still feel the thrust of Paul's words to Timothy: 'preach the word; be urgent, in season and out of season. . . .' (2 Timothy 4:2.)

The second thing is that the method was itself important. Paul uses other methods of putting over the gospel as well. In 2 Corinthians 5:11 he says, 'Knowing therefore the fear of the Lord, we persuade men,'. Later in the same chapter he speaks of 'beseeching' people. In Acts we find that Paul 'argued' about the gospel (17:2, 17; 18:4, 19; 19:8). In Acts 19:9 it appears that this took the form of public debate in the style of the philosophers of the day. But the spread of the gospel is still specially associated with 'preaching'. God still pleases to save men through the 'foolishness of what is *preached*' (1 Corinthians 1:21).

One reason at least for this may be seen through an incident of my own experience which is by no means uncommon. I remember at one time having long discussions about the Christian faith with someone I knew very well. In this particular case, I found these debates becoming more and more frustrating. I never seemed to be able to clinch a line of argument; there were constant misunderstandings of each other's language, and the constant output of red-herrings left us exhausted. Since the other person had no desire to convert me, this was more exhausting for me than him! Eventually, I got desperate. I said, 'Look: let me just have a go at telling you simply what the gospel really is and what it implies. After that we'll discuss it.' So he sat quiet while I told the old old story. At the end, he said, 'If *that* is what you are talking about, then there is very little I would want to quarrel with.' The discussion that followed was on a completely different level.

What I had actually done was to ask him if I could preach to him. Preaching is an authoritative presentation of the message:

an 'open statement of the truth' (2 Corinthians 4:2). The fact
is that the gospel is not just something that is true because it
can be supported by an argument. It is truth; in the end it can
only carry conviction because it just 'is'. At one time men used
to argue that large objects would fall to the ground at a faster
speed than small objects. Then Galileo did an experiment from
the leaning tower of Pisa. Anyone who received a description of
this experiment could not go on using the old arguments in the
same way. Objects all fall at the same speed (apart from the
question of wind-resistance). It is the truth of the matter. It
just 'is' so. Once you accept that, then your whole reasoning
process is changed.

Preaching confronts people with the gospel as a total fact to
be reckoned with; and there is no substitute for it.

In addition, it is apparently possible for the word of God to go
forth without the Spirit. Some New Testament language implies
this anyway. If the message was automatically backed up by the
Spirit, then to remark on such a fact would be pointless. But the
Scripture indicates a number of possible ways in which the
message would not be backed up by the Spirit.

One is indicated by Jesus's temptation in the desert. The devil
can quote scripture, so that God will then not own it. Peter says
that the scriptures can be twisted to destructive ends (2 Peter
3:16).

Another way is the motivation of the preacher. Paul sees it
possible for preachers to 'preach themselves'; to use the gospel
to further their own influence over others. This is a real temptation to any preacher who has a natural gift, as a communicator,
especially if he also has a certain personal magnetism. Paul
turned his back on this. It is not that he sought to be a non-
entity. In fact, in the second epistle to Corinth he devoted a good
deal of time to maintaining his apostolic authority. But he was
only there to serve – 'ourselves your servants for Jesus's sake'
(2 Corinthians 4:5). Even Paul and Apollos could not help having
'supporters' (1 Corinthians 1:12), but it is quite another thing to
use the gospel for that purpose. Paul knew that this would
'empty the cross of its power' (1 Corinthians 1:17).

A third factor is the attitude of the preacher to methods used in his task. Paul deliberately avoided the usual rhetorical devices and logical contortions common in his day. For him the power of the message did not depend upon such tricks. All he had to do was to make the truth clear and the Spirit would demonstrate and empower it (1 Corinthians 2:4–5). By a strange irony he unconsciously produced a new and far superior kind of rhetoric. You only have to read Romans 6, or 8, or 1 Corinthians 1:10–25 to feel the sheer literary strength of it. Paul had no cult of deliberate ugliness. For him everything had to serve the message, so that, as he says, 'your faith might not depend upon human wisdom, but on God's power' (1 Corinthians 2:5).

The Spirit and witness

Luke's account of Jesus's teaching after his resurrection stresses the task of witness (Luke 24:48; Acts 1:8). Here the Spirit is referred to as giving the power to witness. In Acts, examples are given of how this actually worked out in practice. For instance, when Peter and John are arrested and brought before the high-priestly committee of inquiry in Acts 4, Peter speaks boldly about the name of Jesus. And we are told (Acts 4:8) that he spoke 'filled with the Holy Spirit'. Now there are passages which speak of people being full of the Holy Spirit as a continuing spiritual state (e.g. Acts 6:3). Something more seems to be indicated in Acts 4:8. For the special situation of menace, the Spirit 'fills' his witnesses in a special way.

There is another side to this. Peter was arrested again, along with other apostles (Acts 5:18, 26–32). On this occasion they gave account of themselves by telling what had been happening, and then added (5:32): 'And we are witnesses to these things, and so is the Holy Spirit whom God has given to those who obey him.' What Peter was saying here was that while people were listening to the words they had been speaking, something else had been going on inside their hearts; the Holy Spirit had also been speaking, corroborating their words. This actually was a fulfilment of something that Jesus himself had promised (John

15:26). The interesting thing is that in that promise, Jesus seems to have been saying that the main witness was borne by the Spirit, and the disciples were 'also' witnesses. In Peter's words the order is reversed!

Witnessing is undoubtedly the basic way in which ordinary believers are called to speak about the gospel. Not all are teachers or preachers; but anyone can be expected to speak of what they have experienced. This is the essence of witness. The word is taken from the law-courts. If you are in the witness-box, then no one wants your opinions, or third-hand evidence, or suppositions, or theories. Nor are you called upon to suggest a verdict. It is your job to state the facts as you have experienced them. The Christian witness has the task of stating the facts of Jesus's death and resurrection *as they have had effect in his experience*: the changes that have taken place in his own life. It is for this task that the Spirit is given to empower the witness.

The Spirit and influence

It is an interesting fact that there are no exhortations in any New Testament epistle for Christians to witness. Certainly in 1 Thessalonians 1:4–10 the Thessalonian Christians are commended for spreading the gospel, and they could hardly do that without witnessing. But it is strange that 'witness' is not referred to even there.

What is noticeable in the passage is the significance of the reference to 'example' and 'faith' as heightening the effectiveness of the word. Peter speaks of the power of God granted to believers whereby they become 'partakers of the divine nature' (2 Peter 1:4). This is a basis for a character development which, Peter says, will keep them fruitful and effective in their knowledge of Christ.

The Spirit is often mentioned in the context of Christian character (e.g. Ephesians 4–5; Galatians 5:16). This in turn is seen as something which especially contrasts with the life of the non-Christian and arouses his interest, curiosity, and even resentment (1 Peter 2:11–17; 4:1–6). There is one case where this is seen as something which might win a person to Christ without a word being said! 1 Peter 3:1 speaks of a wife winning an unconverted husband. In a society where women were not expected to take the initiative such a policy would be much more likely to be effective than talkative 'witnessing'. In brief, Peter says that the husband may be won by the modesty of his wife, and by what we should now call her 'good taste' in the way she dressed! (Her attitude towards personal appearance was, in fact, to be equivalent to Paul's attitude towards the act of preaching.)

This does not mean that Christians were to be strictly reticent about their faith: far from it. But they were not to be noisily indiscriminate about their witness. There are two texts that *do* speak of how Christians should speak: 1 Peter 3:15, and Colossians 4:6. Both exhort the believer to be prepared to speak when called upon. He is to be 'wise', to have answers ready. And both of the texts speak of 'giving an answer'. The assumption is that the non-Christians will ask questions ... that our lives will arouse their respectful curiosity. Maybe we feel obliged to be vocal about our faith sometimes because our lives have no influence. It is doubtful whether such witness is backed up by the witness of the Spirit. Certainly harm is sometimes done by 'ramming' religion down people's throats, though this must not be confused with the loving enthusiasm of people who are aglow with God's love in their hearts and cannot help talking about it.

The Spirit and mission

The promises of the risen Lord to his disciples have a kind of urge, a thrust about them. Although very many Christians of every age have never had opportunity or call to go further than their native town, the Holy Spirit has always tended to enlarge their vision and broaden their horizon. The church is equipped to witness to Christ 'in the uttermost parts of the earth' (Acts 1:8); to 'preach the gospel to every creature' (Mark 16:15), and to 'make disciples of all nations' (Matthew 28:19). There is therefore a cosmopolitanism about the Spirit. This has two effects at least in the life of the church.

First, it affects the thinking and prayers of the believers. They dare not limit their interest in the spread of the gospel. Even if their bodies do not travel, their thoughts and prayers and generosity will. Churches without this spirit die. I remember preaching once in a small mission hall one Easter Sunday. There were only about twenty people there, and I noticed that the building was well barricaded against vandals. But the presence of God was exciting, to put it mildly. Over the lunch table my hosts apologized for the smallness of the numbers. Several of their members were, they explained, preaching in other churches that day. Then it also transpired that in a matter of a few years over half a dozen young people had gone from the congregation to serve Christ abroad with the gospel, partly at least supported by that tiny fellowship! I compared it with some churches I knew with several hundred in a morning congregation from which no missionary had gone for years. . . .

For the other effect in the church's life will be that some will be called by the Spirit to go abroad with the gospel. There is, of course, a certain romanticism about going abroad, but we are not talking of that here. The fact is that since Pentecost there has always been a cross-cultural movement of the gospel. Even Jesus had to go to Tyre and Sidon once in his earthly life (Mark 7:24), despite his clearly defined mission. Peter was the apostle to the Jews (Galatians 2:7), yet found himself dealing with Gentiles (Acts 10) and his first letter is sent to Jewish Christians living among the Gentiles 'abroad'. This is partly, at least, connected with a feature noted earlier; the way the Spirit defies all cultural barriers.

But it has a positive side, too. The fact that Gentiles (i.e. 'foreigners' to the Jews) could be Christians without giving up being Gentiles implied God's willingness to accept and bless non-Jewish cultures and life-styles. It did not mean that God tolerated immorality or injustice should these be prevalent in a culture, but it did mean that vastly different ways of behaving in society, and quite different ways of looking at life, could be vehicles of the work of the Spirit. It is a sort of reversal of the tower of Babel. There was to be no stereotyping, making everything the same. The Spirit was to make all these differences expressions of the 'multi-coloured grace of God' (1 Peter 4:10). And since every local church is, in a way, to be a sample of the church universal, the Spirit is always tending to develop such a cosmopolitan outlook in each fellowship. As the Spirit is a 'first instalment' of the End, so we are to have a foretaste here of that magnificent vision of it in the book of Revelation (7:9):

> And I looked, and behold, a great multitude which no man could number, from [still, even in heaven] every nation, from all tribes and peoples and tongues, standing before the throne and before the Lamb. . . .

7

THE SPIRIT OF GRACE: 1

Readings: John 3; Isaiah 6; Job 42:1–5; Romans 9–10.

'Grace' is a colossal word in the Bible. The meaning ranges from 'pleasantness' to 'God's salvation'. Someone has defined its highest meaning as 'God's favour at work when it is most needed and least deserved'. In a rather grim passage in Hebrews (10:29), the Holy Spirit is called 'the Spirit of grace', that is the Spirit who carries out God's loving designs for the well-being of those who belong to Christ. This leads us straight on to look at the way the Spirit works in the experience of individual human beings. Some general points need to be dealt with first.

To begin with, there is a great need for caution in trying to establish doctrines about this subject. God made human beings in his image, and that means that each one shares something of his uniqueness. No two people have quite the same experience of life. The Spirit tends to overcome the drab 'sameness' that sin fosters in our lives, and makes us real individuals. But at the same time, when the Spirit works within a human being he becomes so closely identified with that person's experience that it is often difficult to sort out where the individual's experience ends and the Spirit's work begins. (This might account for a similar problem in Scripture, in John's gospel, of deciding where the words of Jesus end, and John's comment on them begins!)

Now the difficulty goes deeper than that. There is a sense in which my experience must have absolute authority for me. I must be true to myself. (This does not mean that I must never do what someone else tells me, or accept someone else's ideas. What it does mean is that if I am not going to be 'phoney', such influences must first become a genuine part of my personal outlook. I must 'identify with it', as people sometimes say.) This is so vital for genuine Christian living that we can become torn between two extremes. One extreme is to discount every kind of Christian experience that does not fit in with ours, or that of the group we belong to. The other is to accept every and any experience as genuine so long as it claims to be Christian.

It is at this point that Scripture has to be a judge; and we have to be careful that our own particular bias to either extreme does not have an unsuspected influence on the way we interpret the Scriptures. What is certain is that we must not make a doctrine out of our own personal experiences. The doctrine comes from Scripture. But personal experiences do provide a certain test of the doctrine. If we develop a doctrine about the work of the Spirit which in fact is not borne out by Christian experience, then we have to go back to the Bible to see what is wrong.

For instance, there has sometimes been teaching that the Spirit can make a believer sinlessly perfect. Such a perfection is never actually demonstrated. Sometimes there has been teaching that holy living or spiritual power only comes through a particular type of religious experience – ecstasy, or vision, or whatever. But there have been people very obviously holy in the Christian sense who have had quite different experiences.

A second general point is that there is a very definite relation between the individual experience and the life of the church. In the first place, there would be no church, for all practical purposes, without individuals. So individual experience is the 'raw material' of the church's life. Each of us has his own contribution to make, however small, to the total life of the church. Some people's contributions are large, for even great decisions of policy and faith still have to be brought into being through individuals. In the New Testament times the mission to the Gentiles had to be carried out through individuals, whether prominent leaders like Paul, or unnamed enthusiasts

like those in Acts 11:20. Either way, it has to be the work of
the Spirit.

On the other hand, the church is more than the sum total
of its members – even of their experience of Christ. A human
body is worth more than the sum total of its components. Someone has calculated that the total value of the chemicals of a
human body is about £3.50. No doubt this will rise with infla-
tion; but the true value of a human being bears no relation to
that! Being part of a human body gives the chemicals a higher
meaning, and so increases their value. The meaning of your individual Christian life is heightened by the fact that it belongs
to the body of Christ, and by what happens in it as a result.
To live 'belongingly' enriches us. We learn from each other; our
sympathies and interests are enlarged and our resolves are
strengthened. We are also regulated and disciplined in the
process. Our individual experience is checked and interpreted as
it comes alongside that of others.

So the outgoing work of the Spirit is a continual interplay
between what we experience within our individual selves and
what he brings into our lives from other believers. The way in
which this works will be considered later.

The Spirit in the world

'While we were yet sinners, Christ died for us.' (Romans 5:8.)
Just as Christ did his work even while mankind was unaware of
what was happening, so the Spirit begins his work in human life
before ever the individual realizes what it is all about. We have
seen something of the way in which the Spirit is at work in the
world of human culture. Something more needs to be said about
this here.

The Bible shows that although some truth about God is
always present in human life, yet, because of his sin, he cannot
help putting up a certain resistance to it. This may be suggested
by God's words before the Flood (Genesis 6:3 AV). But Jesus's
words make this clearer in John 16:8–11. Here he asserts that
the basic activity of his Spirit in the world will be to bring

home the reality of sin and righteousness and judgement to people in such a way that they have to face it for themselves (the full meaning of the word 'convince' or 'convict').

One thing that is easily overlooked in understanding this rather difficult passage is that everything is related to Jesus himself. Basically what is said here is that the Spirit forces people to face spiritual realities by bringing them face to face with Jesus himself. Everywhere, where people know the sound of the word 'Jesus', the Spirit is 'striving' in this direction. Missionaries speak of situations in which, after proclaiming the gospel, someone comes to them and says, 'I knew there must be a God like that somewhere.' Many years ago, after visiting Bhatgaon, a town some miles from Kathmandu in Nepal, I spoke with a missionary of the feeling of oppression I had felt there. 'Yes,' she said, 'it is a strange thing, but when we first went there the people could not possibly have known what the word "Jesus" meant. It might as easily have been a brand of detergent. Yet we found an almost instinctive resistance to the very name.' Nobody can come to faith in Christ without this prior conflict in his spirit in some form or another. The clearer the Holy Spirit's witness to Christ becomes, the more open becomes the resistance. In the history of God's chosen people this becomes especially obvious, so that in Stephen's last address before his martyrdom he says to the Jews, going through their long history, 'You always resist the Holy Spirit,' (Acts 7:51).

The call of God

Almost the last words of the Bible, in the book of Revelation, deal with the way the Spirit speaks to man, calling him to faith in Christ. This is linked with the message of the 'fellowship of the Spirit' – 'The Spirit and the Bride say, "Come." ' (Revelation 22:17.) So the message of Jesus himself when on earth is the same message today, for he said, 'Come to me'. To some extent, then, we can see how that invitation is brought to man by seeing how Jesus made his invitation.

It was an invitation which people might hear as individuals

(e.g. John 4:10, 14) and also as members of a larger group being
addressed generally (John 7:37). Very many different means
were used. The facts of everyday life were used, giving simple
things a new significance. Sowing and reaping, fishing, losing
and finding, housework, were all made to speak of the kingdom
of God. So today people are sometimes awakened to spiritual
issues by a sunset, a problem, a baby's laugh, or some similar
small circumstance.

Another means was the word of Scripture. Jesus said that they
testified of him (John 5:39) and that his own words 'were spirit'
which should draw people to believe (John 6:63–64).

Yet another means was the symbolism of public worship.
Jesus takes the ceremony of pouring out the water from Siloam
at the Feast of Tabernacles as a picture of the gift of his Spirit
(John 7:37–39). Miracles could be used to arrest people's attention and illustrate vividly Christ's own offers and claims (John
6:25–35). He used his own disciples to spread the message
(Matthew 10, Luke 10); and this of course is found after Pentecost as a kind of chain reaction (1 Thessalonians 1:5–7). A
special example of that is found in John 1:46, where Philip finds
Nathanael and quells his scepticism by the simple invitation,
'Come and see.'

Perhaps the most remarkable means of all was that by which
Christ came to people as someone in need of help. A Samaritan
woman is drawn to him in the first place by an unexpected
request for a drink of water. This gave her the confidence to
begin asking questions. Peter was called into full discipleship
after being asked for the loan of a boat. So it is that people have
been drawn to Christ in the first instance by being asked to help
with, say, something like the redecorating of the church. One
person I know became a Christian through being asked along to a
Bible class as an escort to her friend: her mother had said she
was not to go alone!

It is clear that this call of the Spirit could come under any
circumstance of life, in failure or success (Matthew 17:17; cf. also
Matthew 11:25–30), in meeting a disciple (Matthew 10:40–41),
or when apparently no one is looking (John 1:48–49), in daily

work (Matthew 4:18–22), or at the height of bitter opposition to Christ (Acts 9:4). There is no knowing where the Spirit may be making his call next.

A problem arises here which has occasioned some long and sometimes sadly bitter debate. Jesus said, 'Many are called, but few are chosen.' (Matthew 22:14.) Does this mean that God calls many people, but does not intend to save them? Other passages, too, suggest that God chooses whom he will save, and his decision is final (Matthew 20:16; Romans 8:30; Acts 13:48). Paul apparently argues that God is sovereign, and can choose whom he will to be lost (Romans 9:14–18). In the same passage Paul insists that God saves people without regard for *any* quality, any quality at all, which might qualify them (Romans 9:16; cf. John 6:65).

But there are other texts which suggest that the responsibility for receiving eternal life rests with man, too. There is a saying put on alarm clocks: 'many are called, but few get up!' Stephen's words in Acts 7:51 show that people do (successfully) resist the Spirit, and that they can be blamed for it. The implication is that they could have yielded to God. The same sort of thinking appears in Hebrews 2:1–3, where men are blameworthy for neglecting such a great salvation. John 3:16 speaks of God loving the whole world, and giving his son for it. A straightforward reading of 1 Timothy 2:4 and Titus 2:11 speaks of God intending the salvation of all men, rather than just choosing some.

These two lines of teaching seem to be contradictory. If God is all-powerful, 'who can resist his will?' (Romans 9:19). But this means that if someone doesn't get saved, he cannot intend them to be. If God is all-loving, how could he intend anyone to be lost if he could save them?

The strange thing about this is that in the Bible itself the teaching about God's love and God's election, about man's responsibility and man's helpless sinfulness, seem to sit side by side quite naturally. The Apostles, who were no fools, do not seem to have felt our problem, or at least not in the same way. This suggests that there is some dimension of the subject which our thinking does not cope with. For instance, an all-loving God does still have to be just. And although it is true that God is all-powerful, the Bible indicates that this is not *sheer* power – it is power 'made perfect in weakness' (1 Corinthians 1:25; 2 Corinthians 12:9). The problem has all the signs of being the sort of paradox that appears in other subjects. For example, the relation between the mind and the brain is a similar problem. Another such paradox is in the two alternative theories of the nature of light, the 'wave' and 'quantum' theories, whereby scientists find themselves in the position of viewing light one moment as a wave, and the next as a particle. Theology is not the only subject with its contradictions.

The best we can do is to lay down a few principles for our thinking.

(1) No answer which excludes some aspect of biblical truth is adequate. To say that God's power is so invincible that man has no choice in the matter defies the biblical assumption that man can and must make choices. (Notice, though, that man's power to choose is a gift from God in the first place.)

(2) No answer can be offered which makes God's power to save as somehow dependent upon man's will. Nobody is saved just by deciding to become a Christian.

(3) No notion of God's power must exclude the possibility that man cannot effectively and finally reject Jesus Christ.

(4) No understanding of God's love must imply that he is ever helpless or indifferent in the face of man's sin.

All this may sound rather negative, but the fact is that we cannot explain this doctrine in a precise and exhaustive way. When the path through a swamp is not very clear, it is important at least to mark out the places where it is not safe to go. What is certain is this: that when the Spirit of God calls in our lives, the first thing to do is not to discuss the theories, but to obey the call. And when we have obeyed the call, no theories about the subject should allow us the faintest whisper of an idea in our minds that this was our doing, and we did quite well after all. It was all the work of the Spirit. Still less should we allow ourselves the thought that this qualifies us to be rather special people.

A new creation

The change that takes place whereby a person becomes a Christian is something so radical, so profound, that the Bible calls it a 'new birth'. As one evangelist used to put it, 'God does not just give you a new start in life; he gives you a new life to start with.'

New birth is not the only term used, however. Paul speaks of it as a 'new creation' in 2 Corinthians 5:17; and he also calls it an adoption in Romans 8. Here the Spirit is called 'the Spirit of adoption, whereby we cry "Abba, Father "' (Romans 8:15 AV). Paul tends to give a different perspective on the gospel from John. John tends to think of the gospel as bringing man into direct personal contact with God as the source of truth and love; an intimate relationship between a father and his son who derives his nature from him. Paul thinks of the gospel as changing a person's status before angels and men; God now publicly owns him as a member of the household rather in the way that formal adoption procedures took place in the ancient world. Putting the two together we can see that we not only become God's children, but the whole universe, 'visible and invisible', is to know it.

Repentance

There are two aspects of this new birth, two sides of the same coin. Repentance is the negative side.

The word is often translated 'a change of mind', but that sounds too casual as it is usually understood. 'Change of attitude' would be better. It involves more than a mere fluctuation in your opinions. It involves a new estimate of yourself altogether. Peter, when confronted with Jesus, said, 'Depart from me, for I am a sinful man, O Lord.' (Luke 5:8.) Not long before he had been half-disposed to argue with Christ (5:5). Isaiah had probably already been a prophet before he saw God in the temple. But then he cried out, 'Woe is me! ... for I am a man of unclean lips,' (Isaiah 6:5). Job protests his innocence and righteousness throughout his sufferings. Then he meets God, and cries, 'wherefore I abhor myself ...' (Job 42:5–6 AV). Judged by human standards we may (justifiably, perhaps) regard ourselves as reasonably decent people. It is only when we see ourselves matched with the 'glory of God' that we take a different view of ourselves. Such a view only takes place as the Spirit of God makes that scathing purity a reality to us.

Such an experience also produces a change of attitude towards the world around us. When the thief on the cross repented, it changed his attitude towards his old companion; he could no longer agree with him. He saw that both of them deserved punishment, whereas probably before then they had both felt they had been fine patriots in joining a revolution. The fact is that there had been a change of values. Sin, that is, wrong done against God (as contrasted with vice, against oneself, or crime, against society) now becomes the most serious problem of life. Inevitably it will involve at the very least attempts to change one's way of life, even though a penitent person despairs of being able to repair the damage. At least he will want to stop making it worse.

Repentance will produce a regret for one's past way of life (Romans 6:21; Luke 18:9–14), and a determination that, some-how, a change must take place (Hebrews 6:1; 1 Peter 1:14–19). This is not merely remorse. Remorse is an inward-looking thing. The remorseful person is really only absorbed with himself, with sadness and shame that he has disappointed his own or others' estimate of himself. Such a person has either to become hardened to the shame of it, or to despair utterly, as Judas did (Matthew 27:3–5; Acts 1:16–18). Ungodly sorrow, says Paul, produces death (2 Corinthians 7:9–10). True repentance is never related solely to the conscience, or to some moral standard, or the standards of others, or to one's own self-respect. These may all be involved, and contribute to the whole. But essentially it is 'repentance towards God' (Acts 20:21). This is why a true penitent, however crushed by guilt and sin, never quite gives up hope, and never loses the dignity of being a human being made in God's image.

In practical experience, this aspect of conversion is very closely related to the atmosphere of thought in which a conversion takes place. As we have seen, the Spirit is the Spirit of the Christian fellowship as well as of the individual. Where a Christian community has lost sight of the holiness of God and his moral demands, repentance in converts may be a rather flimsy affair; though God does sometimes unveil his holy presence unexpectedly. What happens more often than not is that the convert goes on, perhaps rather weakly, in Christian experience until the reality of the Lord to whom he has become committed dawns on him more fully. Repentance then appears as a belated fruit of the Spirit.

Repentance may not manifest itself in very obviously emotional expressions of sorrow. Some people do not express themselves in that way. Some people's sin as it appears before God is not particularly in the moral sphere of life at all. It may be intellectual; wrong thinking about God is, after all, just as damning as wrong action. But repentance always involves the determination that life must, at all costs, change direction. As such, repentance is spoken of in scripture as bestowed by God (Acts 11:18; 2 Timothy 2:25). It is Christ's gift (Acts 5:31), the end result of that work of the Spirit in the world which we have seen referred to in John 16:8–11. This fact, that repentance is God's work, does have this comfort: that if as Christians we feel that we do not really begin to see ourselves as God sees us, we can with confidence beseech God to deal with us until we do. Though the result could be rather harrowing....

Faith in Christ

The text which speaks of repentance as 'towards God' goes on to speak of salvation as by 'faith in our Lord Jesus Christ' (Acts 20:27). In a way, this is inevitable. Genuine repentance leaves no way out of the distress but trust in Jesus Christ. Faith in Christ is no mere intellectual assent to some doctrinal statements, though something has to be said about him. He must at least be known as the risen 'Lord' (Romans 10:9). Nor can its reality be measured by the intensity of emotion present at the time. Nor is it simply a decision to be a Christian. Faith is the full commitment of the person to Jesus Christ (Acts 8:37; Roman 6:3–8). It takes the form of what the Bible calls a *covenant* (e.g. 1 Corinthians 11:25) in which the believer enters into something like a contract which is eternally binding. The believer commits himself, sins and all, to Jesus Christ as his Lord. God, on the other hand, undertakes to forgive his sins, to accept him freely, and to grant him a new life whereby he is enabled to know God and to serve him.

This new life is the work of the Spirit (2 Corinthians 5:15; Acts 2:38; Romans 8: 1–17). Believing is spoken of as 'coming to Christ' (Matthew 11:28; John 6:37), that is, leaving the old state of heart and mind, and entering into a new one in which Christ is the all–important reality. It is a response to Christ's own invitation, which is itself the work of the Spirit (John 6:63–65). In so far as a person may not be able to feel or appreciate the reality of Christ, it involves treating him as if he were a reality, until eventually he shows himself as such (compare faith in prayer in Mark 11:24, and the waiting for the Spirit before Pentecost). The resurrection appearances of Christ all have as one aspect of them the idea that Jesus Christ is present with us by his Spirit whether we realize it or not. Faith involves believing that and living by it.

Such a commitment of faith also involves 'confession'; Romans 10:9 says:

> if you confess with your lips that Jesus is Lord, and believe in your heart that God has raised him from the dead, you will be saved....

'Confession' is normally thought of as owning up to something one has done wrong. The Bible word certainly has the idea of 'coming clean'. No believer can pretend not to be a believer in-definitely. But it also has a rather more positive idea. The word is used to refer to what a person did when he called upon his god. To call upon a god meant that you expected the god to respond to your devotion. So by calling upon him you became identified in the eyes of other people as a worshipper of that particular god. To 'call upon the name of the Lord Jesus' meant that you worshipped him in such a way that other people would come to see that you were committed to him. In the early church this was normally done by an adult convert undergoing baptism (Acts 2:38, 41; Romans 6:3) and from then on the outward worship which marked him off as a Christian was in the way he shared with others in the 'breaking of bread'. In this the Christians 'proclaimed the Lord's death' (1 Corinthians 11:26). The simplest form of 'confession' seems to have been 'Jesus is Lord' (Romans 10:9; Colossians 2:6; Philippians 2:11; cf. Acts 8:37). In 1 Corinthians 12:3 Paul says that no one can do this (and mean it) 'except by the Holy Spirit'.

8

THE SPIRIT OF GRACE: 2

Readings: Romans 6; 1 John 1:1–9; 1 John 5; Ephesians 1; 1 Corinthians 2:14 – 3:9.

New life

When repentance and faith come, God pledges himself to bring about a new life in the believer. This is a characteristic work of the Spirit. He is the 'Spirit of life in Christ Jesus' (Romans 8:2). In many churches on Sundays Christians still declare in the words of the ancient Nicene Creed: 'I believe in the Holy Spirit, the Lord, the giver of life.'

To understand what takes place we need to use the picture language of metaphors. None of them will show us the whole truth. Taken in isolation any one of them can be misleading. But some are more typical of the Bible than others.

Most of us tend to have a picture of 'life' as a 'something' that exists inside us – the 'ghost in the machine'. Take the 'ghost' away, destroy it, and you have death. Put one back, and you have life. Now although this picture is used very occasionally in Scripture, it is not typical. In Genesis 2:17, God said to Adam concerning the fruit of the tree of knowledge of good and evil, 'in the day that you eat of it you shall die'. But Adam and Eve did not become corpses on the day that they sinned. Even what you might call 'the spiritual part of them' did not die: they could still converse with God (Genesis 3:9–13). Dying and living are, in Scripture, more a matter of *relationships* and *function*. Their relationship of trust with God began to die; 'life' became a matter of making excuses, and shifting responsibility, even blaming God (Genesis 3:12–13). So the way they responded to God, the way they functioned as beings made in God's image, began to die.

This in turn means that the relationship between each element of the human make-up, between the inner life of the spirit and the physical life of the body, also begins to break up, and so the whole person is dying. New life means the reversal of all that. There is a new relationship of confidence with God. The Spirit makes it possible for us to be 'alive to God in Christ Jesus' (Romans 6:11) – notice the stress on the relationship, 'to God'; to be alive 'according to the flesh', says Paul in Romans 8:13, is death!

This means that the Christian begins to function as a human being in a completely new way. All the New Testament writers see the work of the gospel as bringing about a state of affairs so new that it is as if God has made a new creation, with a new Adam and a new humanity. This is because of the way the cross has dealt with sin.

If we go back to the original Adam in Genesis 1 and 2, it is clear that before the Fall his life could fairly be called sinlessness; his obedience to God was perfect. After the Fall, with but one exception, 'there is no man who does not sin' (1 Kings 8:46; cf. Hebrews 4:15). This includes Christians as well. The new birth does not make Christians sinless. Sometimes it has been taught that Christians could have a lesser kind of perfection – perfect love for God; but this idea has died 'the death of a thousand qualifications'. Christians just don't have any kind of perfection in themselves. The more spiritually sensitive they are, the more (if they think about themselves) they are aware of this fact.

So far, then, the history of the human race offered two alternatives only. One was sinless perfection, the other the life of the sinner, out of touch with God, either individually or communally self-centred, inevitably under God's condemnation, and unable and unwilling to get in touch with the only power that could do anything for him.

Now when Christ died on the cross, he bore the death consequent upon our sin. 'The wages earned by sin is death, but the
gift God gives is eternal life.' (Romans 6:23.) Jesus Christ
actually received the 'wages' due to us. He died, 'the just for the
unjust' (1 Peter 3:18). He gave 'his life a ransom in the place
of many' (Mark 10:45). Among many other things, two are most
important for us. One is that this death dealt with the penalty of
sin. Once and for all it was made possible to face up to sin and
not be afraid of its penalty. It was possible to have sinned, and
yet not to be barred from fellowship with God. The other equally
important thing is that such a pardon gave full due to God's own
word, 'the soul that sins shall die'. His death for sin has become
my death; the Holy Spirit has made that cross my cross. So a new
kind of life emerges. It is not sinless. But nor is it merely
sinning, a life in which sin is free to exercise its power and
penal consequences in death. It is a life in which God has a
pardoning relationship with me, while I am yet someone in
whom sin still is at work. And this pardon is something I can
never presume on, never take for granted. It is a pardon that
constantly exposes sin in me as unbearably evil, because it comes
'cross-shaped' to me; based upon Christ bearing the punishment
of sin on the cross.

The result is that a new kind of living begins. One of the most
helpful illustrations I know came to me from St. Marylebone
parish church in North London, where at one time I used to
go for times of prayer. It helped me because at the time I felt
that my whole Christian life was in ruins, and I was near despair.
I glanced across at this particular window, attracted by its
beauty. Then I was puzzled by the curiously jumbled design –
there seemed to be bits of trees, and arms and legs distributed
haphazardly all over. Then I noticed an inscription. It said that
this had been made up from the shattered fragments of a window
that had been destroyed during the blitz on London; and it
was in memory of those in the parish who had fallen in the war.
Gradually it dawned on me that the ruined pieces of a window
now had a new and higher meaning than ever the original had:
they had been fashioned into a memorial of heroism and sacri-

fice. Likewise God takes the shattered pieces of life ruined by sin and rebuilds them into monuments of his pardoning grace (Ephesians 1:6–12).

It is this that Paul means when he talks in his letter to the Romans about 'being justified by grace' (3:24), 'justified by his blood' (5:9), and 'justified by faith' (3:28, 5:1). Justification is his technical word for this transforming forgiveness. The ruined past is not annihilated; it is accepted and refashioned as a living expression of the mercy that comes from the cross. And so we are born again, not as sinlessly perfect, not as sinners to whom sin is second nature, but 'justified', given a new, pardoned relationship with God through which his Spirit can work in our lives in spite of our sins.

New living

Birth by the Spirit of God is only the beginning; but it is a beginning, and the Christian life afterwards goes on by the same principle. John says, 'Let what you heard from the beginning abide in you.' (1 John 2:24.) He insists that what happens at conversion becomes the pattern for the rest of a Christian's life (1 John 1:7–9).

> If we walk [continuous living] in the light, as he is in the light, ... the blood of Jesus his Son goes on cleansing us from all sin.

Paul says in Colossians 2:6, 'As you therefore received Christ Jesus as Lord, so go on living in him. . . .'

But in fact we find this very difficult to believe. There is an almost universal instinct among us to think that once we are converted then the Spirit gives us the strength to keep it up, to keep the rules, to conform to whatever pattern of life we are led to believe is a Christian one. This becomes the standard of being a 'good Christian'. Paul's reaction to this is quite devastating. Writing to the Galatians he said passionately (Galatians 3:2–3):

> Let me just ask you this: did you receive the Spirit by doing the works of the Law, or by hearing with faith? Can you be so silly? Having started in the Spirit, are you now completing the affair by human effort?

Of course the trouble is that it seems almost immoral to live like that. Paul says that some 'slanderously charged' him with saying, 'why not do evil that good may come?' (Romans 3:8). Against this he insists that the gospel, so far from undermining the Law of God for man's life, is the only way of upholding it (Romans 3:31). This is because Paul asserts that when a person commits himself to Christ the Holy Spirit so links him to Christ that his old relationship with sin is broken; it is a death (Romans 6:3):

> Do you not know that all of us who have been baptized into Christ Jesus were baptized into his death?

This is the foundation for the new life.

Union with Christ

From time to time the idea of union with Christ has come up already; and in considering the new birth it has become quite prominent. To our strongly individualistic and materialistic ways of thinking in the western world the whole idea presents real difficulties. How can a person 'die with Christ', and how can we talk about 'being risen with him'?

We had best begin by noting the way in which the Bible speaks of it. First of all, this kind of relationship works in two ways. The Bible talks of Christ's union with his whole church, and it also speaks of Christ and the individual believer. Much the same principles apply to both, though the second one is dealt with in more detail.

One picture is taken from a building and its cornerstone (Ephesians 2:20–22; Colossians 2:7; 1 Peter 2:4–8). Here the main idea is that Christ is indispensable to the church throughout its entire history. If at any time it were without Christ, it would collapse whatever wealth, organization or power it might display.

Another picture is taken from analogies of living things: the plant and the root (Colossians 2:7); the branch and the vine (John 15:1–5); and especially the body and the head (1 Corinthians

6:15; 12:12; Ephesians 1:22–23; 4:15–16; 5:29–30). The first two emphasize that the life and energy come from Christ. The last one emphasizes the fact that the power of the body to function intelligently as a unity and to express Christ's mind in the world depends on union with him. Only when Christians see that Christ and *only* Christ is what makes a church a true church is there likely to be unity of thought and action among them. It follows of course for the individual believer that to belong to Christ means to belong to his body, the church.

A more personal analogy is found in the Lord's Supper. Here the idea is that we receive life and energy from eating food, so we receive life and energy for our God-ward life by trusting Christ. Jesus himself rescues us from thinking that there is any sense in which we 'eat' him by eating the sacramental bread: he insists that his words 'are spirit', and that he gains his life from the Father in the same way as we draw life from him (John 6:53–58) – by faith.

Another analogy, even more important for the individual aspect, is that of the union of wife and husband. Here the idea of a union of love is prominent, in which the two become in some respects 'one flesh' and yet each preserves a distinct identity. An important secondary idea is that of the status which the husband gives the wife in marriage; he takes on any legal claims made against her (Romans 7:1–4; Ephesians 5:31; Revelation 19:7; 22:17). So Jesus pays all the 'debts' incurred by my wrong-doing.

Two other analogies come very close together, and again are highly significant. One is the union of an individual with a community (1 Corinthians 10:16; 2 Corinthians 13:4; Acts 2:42). This is so influential that sometimes when Paul uses the phrase 'in Christ' there is almost a suggestion of its meaning 'in the church' (1 Corinthians 4:10–15; Galatians 3:28; Colossians 1:2). The other is the union of a race with its ancestor. Our union with Adam means that we are sinners. But by the same token, we can be united with Christ who died for sin, and this means that our sin has been 'died for'.

This great variety of language about our union with Christ is reinforced by three great phrases especially found in Paul's letters: 'Christ in', 'Christ with' and 'in Christ'. This should lead us to realize that the whole idea is no simple one to be understood with a few slick phrases; it means that Jesus Christ is the permanent principle, company and environment of living. It is a living union which grows as we grow with a life derived from the very union itself (Ephesians 5:29–30). It is an intimate personal union in which each believer has a communion with Christ as unique as that between a husband and wife; and in which the believer's character develops in a growing likeness to the Saviour (John 14:23–24; Ephesians 5:31). It is this, and not some incommunicable ecstasy, which makes it 'the mystical union' as it is sometimes called.

What happens, then, is that the Spirit brings us into a living unity with Christ in such a way that at one and the same time we become more truly individuals and more fully members of each other in the body of Christ. There is no stereotyping process, even though churches often try to impose one. Nor is there any room for isolation, even if we wanted it. When one member suffers, we all suffer, whether we want it or not, or even believe it or not. This is largely because this kind of communion is not based on what goes on inside us. It is based on something objective, outside us, begun in eternity, carried out in history – the coming, the death and the resurrection of Jesus Christ.

This union is repeatedly spoken of as the work of the Holy Spirit. That means that however we think of it we must do so in terms of everything we have seen that Scripture teaches about the Spirit. Christ dwells in us by the Spirit of God indwelling (Romans 8:9–10). The Christian's inner strength is by the Spirit – 'Christ dwelling in your hearts by faith' (Ephesians 3:17). Our experience of being God's children is by the Spirit of his Son (Galatians 4:5–6). God dwells in his people as in a temple, by his Spirit (1 Corinthians 6:17–20; Ephesians 2:22). And last but not least, the Spirit makes the fact that Christ lives in us something which is really effective and unmistakable in our lives (1 John 3:24; 4:13).

On the whole, I think that it is impossible to imagine what

this union is really like. What happens is that you look back on Christian life after a while, and begin to recognize the marks of it. In any present moment of time, it is about as hard to see as the back of your own eyeball....

Sanctification [See also Appendix 1]

Historically, this has been another battle-ground. Much of the unnecessary controversy will, I hope, have been avoided by approaching the subject this late in the book.

There are two aspects to sanctification. One is the idea of being set apart for God's use. Buildings, clothing, vessels, were sanctified in this way in the Bible, as well as human beings. In general, the Bible connects this first aspect of sanctification with the application of sacrificial blood, and in this sense, too, Christians are 'saints', 'sanctified by the blood of Christ' (1 Corinthians 1:2; Hebrews 10:29). But things are not made in the image of God; human beings are. Human beings have this inner life of thought, motivation and will which has to be sanctified. This aspect of the matter is more clearly connected with the work of the Holy Spirit. How is our inner experience 'sanctified'?

The first thing to recall is the fact that whatever happens after conversion, it has to take place by the same principle as the conversion itself. We go on as we begin – by faith, in the Spirit, trusting Christ, according to his word.

Now going on inevitably means persistence, keeping up the same policy. The Christian at his conversion has to give up all hope of getting any commendation from God by keeping the rules of the Law – even God's law, let alone any of his own making. In the same way he then has to live the Christian life. But the law is still present in the background. It still warns the Christian when he is tempted, and it still pronounces upon his sins. Paul speaks of the law as acting as a 'pedagogue' (Galatians 3:24, Greek). In the ancient world children were committed into the care of a slave who looked after them and educated them, or took them to be taught by someone else. Once they were old enough they were of course free from his jurisdiction. Now one can easily imagine situations in which a young boy would claim his freedom, and then misbehave himself. His father might well say, 'Since you are acting like a child, I shall have to treat you like one,' and send him back to his pedagogue. The law acts like that for the Christian. If he tries to live his own life, either by going his own way or by 'working to rule', the Law gets to work, leading him back to Christ by making him aware that something is going wrong. But the law has another function, too, as part of God's word.

If the Christian is not to live by the rules of law, then what is he to live by? The Bible's answer is by faith in Christ. As he called Christ 'Lord' and so in principle committed every interest of his life to Christ at his conversion, so day by day, and on any occasion when significant decisions have to be made, he must commit the concerns of the particular step to be taken to the Lord Jesus Christ. If he has a sense of guilt or failure, he must bring this to the Lord, by penitent faith, just as he did when this life began. Conversion is like the first night of the play; the rest of life is acting it out at every step, every crisis. The plot remains the same, though as any actor will tell you, every performance is unique. But whatever happens, good or bad, it has to be faced before the Lord. Abraham had to live like that: 'Walk before me, and be thou perfect,' said the Lord (Genesis 17:1, AV), and that was the only perfection possible to him. John, towards the end of the New Testament, says the same sort of thing (1 John 1:7–8). The principle is expressed in Hebrews thus: 'run the race ... looking to Jesus' (Hebrews 12:1–2).

The most helpful picture I know comes from when I learnt to plough. The first time I tried it, I watched the plough and the horses(!), and they seemed hopelessly uncontrollable. The ploughman had a good laugh at my efforts. Then he went to the far end of the field, waved a rather well-used handkerchief and said, 'Keep your eye on this.' It was the hardest thing in the world to forget the plough and the furrow, and I did not entirely succeed. But the result was infinitely better, and I had learnt the secret of progress. Did I thereby abandon the idea of getting a straight furrow? No, I was fulfilling it! (See Romans 3:31.)

Now the law, along with the rest of God's word, does this vital thing; it tells me where to find that 'mark of God's high calling in Christ Jesus' (Philippians 3:14) and how to recognize it.

But something else has to be said to be fair to this subject. Many people do insist that at some time after their conversion they had a second experience of Christ by the Spirit which was almost like a second conversion. This seems to happen especially in times of revival. There is some degree of support for this idea in Scripture, even when many texts that are cited are explained away. 1 Corinthians 3:1 speaks of Christians on two levels, 'carnal' and 'spiritual', and something of the same idea appears in Romans 8:4–13. Romans 6:3 speaks of Christians who clearly do not know what has happened to them; and the exhortation in Romans 12:1–2 shows that a person could be a Christian and yet not wholly dedicated to the Lord.

Now there is no doubt that if a person's Christian life is mainly governed by selfish or merely human considerations (i.e. 'carnal'), something pretty radical has got to happen for them to be spiritual. Discovering what it is to be 'crucified with Christ' is a traumatic experience. A total dedication of one's life to God is undoubtedly a crisis for a Christian. And the point is that none of that can take place without the Spirit. It is after all doubtful whether a life in which these things have not happened could really be called '*filled* with the Spirit', however keen and loving and enthusiastic it might be. Of course, there is no reason why such things should not be elements of a normal conversion. The point is that often they are not, and then something more has got to happen for the injunction of Ephesians 5:18 – 'keep on being filled with the Spirit' – to be really possible. To this extent a second experience (and maybe more) will be needed for a Spirit-filled life, one in which the Spirit has free course. Until this takes place, growth is always going to be hindered by prejudice, self-will, and what James calls 'double-mindedness' (James 1:7).

The Spirit at work in the believer will then produce growing effects in his life. He will grow in grace and understanding of

Christ (2 Peter 3:18). Christian character, instead of being rather artificially cultivated (who has not suffered from the 'Hallelujah grin'?), grows spontaneously like fruit on a tree (Galatians 5:22), and prayer is taken out of the realm of a devotional performance into a heart-cry to God which prevails with him even when words cannot be found (Romans 8:26; cf. Ephesians 6:18). Rules of life which a Christian may use to help him serve the Lord best now find their proper place in life (Romans 14:14–23; 1 Corinthians 9:19). The believer gets to recognize God at work in his life, and to act more confidently in reliance on that work. He is open to the infinite variety of the Spirit's work, 'anointing' him for particular tasks (2 Corinthians 1:21–22; Acts 13:4), filling him in special ways at times of emergency (Acts 4:8; 13:9), filling him unexpectedly with fresh vision or sudden joy (Acts 7:55; 13:52), and so on. In particular he will find that there are occasions when his life and service will be fraught with the presence of God in power; and some Christian workers have this as a constant feature of their ministry.

It is claimed by some Christians that this is bestowed by a 'baptism in (or of) the Holy Spirit', which is normally accompanied by speaking in tongues. The phrase used is certainly ambiguous, since the only certain meaning of it in Scripture (1 Corinthians 12:13) is applied to *all* Christians – the new birth. The biblical argument is not water-tight enough for the idea to be a dogma. There is, I think, at least a practical truth in it. Many people certainly do find it possible to act in faith on the reality of the miraculous and supernatural elements of the Spirit's work through an experience of what is certainly the most elementary of the 'gifts'.

Christian certainty

In chapter 2 we saw that we cannot be made certain of God by 'proofs' in the way we can of other things. The Spirit confronts us with him. From this comes the Christian confidence that we can, in some instances at least, be sure of God. In two areas this has always been of special concern to Christians. One is that

of assurance of salvation; the other is in guidance. We may know
that we are of God (1 John 5:19 – it is a theme of the whole
epistle); the matter is clinched for us by the Spirit (Ephesians
1:13–14). And we may know 'what is that good, acceptable and
perfect will of God' (Romans 12:2): there are outstanding
examples of the Spirit's guidance in Acts, especially Acts 16:6–7.
The principles behind the sense of certainty are the same in both
areas. They derive from the very nature of the Spirit's work as
we have seen it.

To begin with, the Spirit's certainty is basically a certainty
about Jesus Christ – his presence, his saving work, his will for
us. He answers questions like, 'Lord, what are you doing with
me?' or, 'What do you want me to do?' rather than, 'What is the
matter with me?' or 'What shall I do next?' The difference is
all-important. His certainty comes as we seek the Lord Jesus
in praying faith.

The Spirit works in us directly, without any intermediary,
so that we meet God first-hand in our inner life. But God never
gives us a relationship 'through the tops of our heads'. He
works through certain means, via certain channels. These means
have a definite relationship to each other. When the relationship
gets confused, trouble follows.

This has to do with the fact that God makes us certain of
himself by the impact of his presence on us as Lord. That is to
say, he exercises his personal authority. The work of the Spirit,
then, is to make that authority effective in our lives. Now he does
this in the various spheres of our life in the world in which he
is present. In the first place, the created world is his work, and
this means that the 'laws of nature' – which are after all God's
laws – have an authority for us. So Jesus ate, and drank, and
slept as his body needed it. He respected the laws governing our
existence. This is roughly what we mean by the guidance of
circumstances and the use of common sense. And yet beyond
those laws there are higher principles sometimes at work which
can only be known by faith, such as enabled Peter to walk on the
water.

These principles governing the way we are to serve God in

this world are expressed in God's word. So the Spirit uses the Scriptures to make known to us the authority of God. But this kind of authority, the authority of *words*, takes on various forms. Probably the clearest example of this is in the government of a nation. Here authority is fundamentally established in the law of the land, its Acts of Parliament, its constitution. At any given moment none of us can argue about this authority; it is just there. We cannot have legal disputes about what part of it we will obey, only about what it means. The Scriptures are like that: they are the fundamental authority for the Christian. If God makes a promise it stands; if he gives a command then the Spirit demands our obedience. Once we know what the words mean, we can be sure of them, on the authority of God, and that sureness is backed by the Spirit.

This is what lies behind the way the New Testament is always referring back to the Old. We can see it at work in passages like 1 John 5:9–12, about our salvation. But as we have seen, the Spirit is the Spirit of the Christian fellowship. Going back to our analogy; government is based on legislature, but it is administered on the whole by the courts. The authority these exercise is entirely dependent on the law. Their business is to administer the law, to expound it, to apply it in particular cases, to ensure that people understand it. The courts are not infallible: a citizen can appeal beyond them. But their authority is real, and in a healthy state will be as good as law for practical purposes. Now the Spirit of God exercises that authority through the church, the people of God. In practice, God makes us sure of himself through the way that his people apply his word to us: 'where two or three are gathered together in my name,' said Jesus, 'there am I in the midst.' (Matthew 18:15–20.)

The idea is further seen in action in 1 Corinthians 5:4 where we get the impression that the Spirit of God is 'waiting in the wings', so to speak. In Acts 8, it appears that the age-long feud between Jews and Samaritans may have made the Samaritans uncertain as to their share in what seemed to be a Jewish salvation (cf. John 4:22). It is as the apostles, representing the young church, laid their hands on Samaritan converts, saying in effect,

'We identify ourselves with you as Christians,' that the Spirit fell upon them, confirming their faith in Jesus.

It is important to remember that this authority is not infallible; it is only rightly exercised subject to the word of God, to which any Christian has the 'right of appeal'. What is more, it is vested in the whole community of God's people, though it may be for practical purposes applied through local congregations, or through representatives duly chosen by them, their pastors and teachers. Expressed another way, the church is God's covenant people, and when they act within the terms of his covenant, then he covenants to make what is said and done effective by his Spirit (cf. Matthew 18:15–18 with John 20:23).

But in the end, we all have to know God for ourselves. In terms of our analogy: the legislation uses the courts to apply its provisions, but the courts have people like the police to carry them out. This is another level of authority, the authority to act. The authority for a believer to act as a Christian, to do something in obedience to God, is the work of the Spirit within his own experience. That is, his own conscience, his own reason, his own motivation. Again, like the police, it is subject to law. Normally that law is known through the courts. So the Spirit in the believer always works according to Scripture, and normally that working comes to us through the fellowship of God's people.

So we see that guidance and assurance normally come within a heart, mind and conscience which have been open to these things: the leading of circumstances, the word of scripture, and the way that scripture is applied by Christian people.

A claim which denies the plain teaching of Scripture about Jesus Christ or his moral demands can be rejected out of hand. As Luther said, 'the conscience is subject to the Word of God.' But beyond that, the leading of the Spirit may be less clear. This much can be said. First, that if a person's conscience is faulty, God's Spirit will always correct it before calling for obedience which might conflict with it (see Peter's experience in Acts 10). Second, that if a Christian feels bound to act, or a Christian leader asks us to act, contrary to the practice or direction of his church, this will always be accompanied by a profound respect for the authority of the church, and a desire to do everything possible to preserve the sense of fellowship with it. Generally speaking, people whose obedience puts them in some conflict with their church do not *walk out* under the leading of the Spirit. What happens is that they continue to seek to serve the church until they are *pushed out* (cf. Galatians 1:11 – 2:10; 1 John 2:19).

We may feel that this is rather unsatisfactory. We would like something more definite, requiring less thought and deliberation. We may not always be sure of what Scripture says, and sometimes we may not feel we get all that much help from our church, even when it is augmented by reading the teaching that has come down to us from the church through the ages.

At this point it is vital to remember two things. The first is that the Spirit who lightens our way is the Spirit of Christ. As we seek to know God, we have to commit everything (especially our desires and prejudices) into the hands of Jesus Christ as the one who died to save us from sin. While we do that as honestly as we can, a time will come when the Spirit of God will bear witness in us, making us *sure* of Jesus (Romans 8:15–16; 1 John 5:6–12, 18–20), whether for salvation, or guidance, or any other need.

This assurance is, in fact, the first taste of the glory of heaven – just a faint beginning. In Ephesians 1:14 the Spirit's 'seal', clinching our trust in Christ, is called the 'guarantee' in the Revised Standard Version. The Greek word, *arrhabon*, had the meaning of 'first instalment' – the down payment to secure a purchase. It was sometimes used of a wedding ring – the assurance that the groom gave to the bride that she was his. And in Hebrews 6:5, believers are said to 'taste of the powers of the age to come'. (This rather difficult passage, incidentally, is saying that so long as a person will not accept the forgiveness found in Christ when he sees it, he cannot find forgiveness anywhere else.)

So how does a person set about being sure of God when some serious question arises? Take the typical example of the need for guidance. First of all, there are the circumstances as they are. It is no use wishing they were different, or waiting for them to change, unless it is clearly our duty to do something about them, in which case we should not ask for guidance when our duty is plain! Then we surrender ourselves afresh to him owning up to anything that troubles our conscience, and we trust him to accept us as we are, overruling what is wrong in us for the sake of Jesus. Then we seek God in his word; he has promised, 'I will guide thee with mine eye,' (Psalm 32:8 AV; 73:24). That means he will guide us whether or not we understand his will or feel we see the way.

This is the second thing to remember. It is more important to have faith that we are being guided than it is to know just what guidance is. We will listen to the teaching of others, especially of other Christians. Often as we pray, think, read and listen, our minds are drawn in a particular direction, our sense of priorities is altered – maybe subtly, maybe quite dramatically. All the time the Spirit is building up a receptivity to his will in our hearts. Eventually, either because circumstances demand it, or because we feel obliged to, we have to decide and act. So we take a step at a time, no more and no less than is necessary, until the going is plain. As we go, we constantly keep ourselves 'under his eye' in a prayerful attitude of trust in the atoning grace of the Saviour, for there will be prejudices, follies, weaknesses, perhaps self-will in us, of which we are not yet aware. But God, who knows the heart, deals with us not according to our spirituality, but because his Son claims us as those for whom he died.

9

THE SPIRIT OF GOD

Readings: John 14–16; Romans 8; 1 Corinthians 2:9–16; 2 Corinthians 3.

The Spirit as a person

It is fairly common nowadays to make the point that the Spirit is not an 'it' but a 'he'. This is certainly important, for a number of reasons. If the Spirit were not personal, then his influence upon us would not be personal; it would be in some way alien to us, artificial. It would be more like a drug, or at the best a kind of hypnotic influence. His control of us would make us less than persons. In actual fact, he makes us more fully and really persons than we ever were; the opportunities offered to us are sometimes a bit unnerving!

He is also the 'Spirit of Christ'. If he were less than personal, we could hardly know Christ as a person. The special characteristics of his personality would be 'filtered out' of the picture. The effect would be rather like reading a computerized love-letter. The bond between us and our Saviour would be reduced to something impersonal, an abstract idea, perhaps, or a principle, or a set of rules, or a pattern to copy. But in fact the Spirit has all the characteristics of a person. The Bible speaks of him as knowing the inner intimacies of God's heart (Romans 8:27; 1 Corinthians 2:11). He makes choices and decisions (Acts 2:4; 1 Corinthians 12:11) and he makes them known to people (Acts 13:2). He teaches, rebukes, in a personal way (John 14:26; 1 Corinthians 2:13; Revelation 2:7; etc.). Ideas can 'seem good' to him; he even prays (Acts 15:28; Romans 8:26). Perhaps most remarkably, the Spirit has feelings: he can be grieved, vexed, and he has love (Ephesians 4:30; Isaiah 63:10; Romans 15:30). Titles that are given him are personal. Imagine calling an *object* a Counsellor (John 14:16), or the Spirit of Jesus (Acts 16:7), or 'Lord' (2 Corinthians 3:17)....

One thing which may have contributed to speaking of the Spirit as 'it' is a peculiarity in the Greek language of the New Testament. Every language has its quirks. One in Greek is that genders of words do not correspond with sex. There are a few cases of this in English, such as calling a ship 'she', but they are quite rare. The Greek word for Spirit, which is *pneuma*, is neuter. (So are some other words for sexed beings, like 'child' or 'sheep'.) For a neuter word, good Greek would always use a neuter pronoun, 'it', leaving the reader to work out whether it might mean 'he'. But in John 14–16 the personal pronoun 'he' is used, and in one text at least this flagrantly breaks the normal rules of grammar (John 16:13).

But the scriptures do provide another reason why he is easily thought of as non-personal. Nearly all the metaphors and symbols are non-personal. ('Counsellor' is the one outstanding exception.) He is never spoken of as a king, or judge, or warrior, as God is when he is being thought of as One. Images used are water, fire, oil, wind, a seal (signet), a dove, and possibly a voice (John 3:5, 8; 7:38; Matthew 3:11, 16; Acts 2:3; Isaiah 61:3; John 6:27; Matthew 10:20; Hebrews 3:7–11). There is a reason for this. Normally when we think of a person, we think of someone to whom we can relate and with whom we can converse 'over against' ourselves. Now the Spirit is not like that *for us* (although he is within the Trinity). As far as I know, there is only one case in Scripture where the Spirit is addressed directly, and it is in a highly mystical and symbolic passage in Ezekiel, where the prophet is bidden to 'prophesy to the wind' (37:9). As John Taylor, in his controversial book on the Spirit *The Go-Between God* (page 43) says, 'You cannot commune with the Holy Spirit, for he *is* communion itself.' To have dealings with the Spirit always means to have dealings with God in Christ. Any attempt to deal with him as a person on his own, so to speak, would result in a kind of spiritistic religious experience.

At this point it is worth comparing the Spirit as a person with other 'spirits'. This is important because sometimes the manifestations of the Spirit seem in scripture to be called 'spirits' (1 John 4:1). Lying spirits can be a sufficiently fair imitation of the Spirit's work for discrimination to be necessary. It is a strange fact that people often find it easier to speak of Satan as 'he' than to speak of the Spirit like that. In actual fact, Satan is really not so fully personal; his activity tends to reduce people to slaves, even robots; he has no real *character* of his own in Scripture. He is a kind of 'silhouette', a negative, destructive imitation of Christ, the spirit of 'antichrist' (1 John 4:3), seeking to displace the real thing. By contrast, the Holy Spirit develops human personality; he has a fully personal character – that of the Lord Jesus Christ, and all the time he is acting on his behalf, not to displace but to exalt him.

The Spirit as God

Generally speaking, the Bible does not go in for formal statements about the nature of the Godhead. The Bible is for the theologian rather like what the natural world is for the scientist. It is the raw material of his thinking. The Bible takes the nature of God largely for granted, and speaks accordingly. There is no explicit statement that 'the Holy Spirit is God'. Even if there were, we should still need to know what the word 'God' meant in such a sentence, for it would mean something quite different to a Hindu or a tribal animist. Apparently plain texts very seldom provide satisfactory proof to convinced opponents, as anyone who has discussed this subject with Jehovah's Witnesses will have discovered. What we see in the Bible is that language is used about the Holy Spirit which can only make sense if he is really the God known in Jesus Christ.

Firstly, the Spirit of the Lord in the Old Testament, otherwise called there the Spirit of God, appears in the New Testament as the Spirit of the Lord, and even the Spirit of Christ. Most of this has already become clear. Now this Spirit is everywhere treated as being identical with God in his functions and status. In the Old Testament whatever the Spirit of God did or said was done or said by God; no distinction is ever made. His qualities are the qualities of God: of omnipresence, of goodness, constancy and power over life (Psalm 139:7; Nehemiah 9:20; Psalm 51:11; Isaiah 40:7). God spoke by the prophets, and their words were his words. These words, no more and no less, were sent by his Spirit (Zechariah 7:12). In the Old Testament, the Spirit is at least as much a part of the being of God as his voice and his breath.

This comes over into the New Testament when it speaks about the Holy Spirit. Like God, he is eternal, infinite, omnipresent, all-knowing, all-powerful (Hebrews 9:14; Acts 2:17; 1 Corinthians 2:10; Luke 1:34–37). His dignity is placed at one point even higher than that of Christ, if such were possible (Matthew 12:32), and to lie against him merits death (Acts 5:1–11). In one text he is solemnly given the title which God the Father shares in common with the Son: 'now *the Lord* is the Spirit' (2 Corinthians 3:17). His divine authority appears in Acts especially (see Acts 10:9–19; 11:12 where he sets aside the Old Testament regulations). As Jesus said in John 3:8, 'the wind (or spirit) blows where it wills,' and no one can dictate to him.

He is constantly referred to as *the* Holy Spirit. That is a way of speaking which assumes that he is unique; it is impossible to see him as even the most important one of a number of holy spirits. He is listed on equal terms with Deity in a large range of passages which are 'trinitarian' in character. Baptism is to be in the name (one name only) of Father, Son and Holy Spirit. The benediction at the end of 2 Corinthians (13:14), faintly reminiscent of the great Old Testament benediction in its threefold form, speaks of benefits from Father, Jesus Christ and the Holy Spirit. There is no sense that the last is an anti-climax, a let-down. The same thing appears in the greeting of 1 Peter 1:2. Paul's writings abound in this kind of language, though it is not always so neatly balanced (Romans 5:1–5; 8:2–3; 1 Corinthians 2:1–4; Galatians 4:4–6; Ephesians 4:4–6; 1 Corinthians 3:16).

We have already seen the way in which Christ, the divine Son, was present on earth by the power of the Spirit. Like God, Jesus was to have 'life in himself', that is, he was not just alive, he was a source of life in the way God is the source of life. His voice was to resurrect the dead (John 5:25–26). Yet the power by which the Son was to have and dispense that life was that of the Spirit of God (regulated by the Spirit, in Romans 1:4, raising the dead by the Spirit, Romans 8:9–11)! The supreme secret of bringing life into existence – not just copying the process in a test-tube – is seen in Scripture as vested in Father, Son and Spirit, quite indiscriminately.

Finally, the Christians of the New Testament made no real distinction between living for God, living in Christ, living by faith, and living in or by the Spirit. The Spirit has just the same absolute unqualified authority in the Christian's life as God, whether God is thought of as the Father or the Son. Now all this appears as part of a faith which stood uncompromisingly for one God as against the 'gods many and lords many' round about (James 2:19; 1 Corinthians 8:5). So what could any being be who had all the attributes and functions of God, but God himself? If he were less than God, then the disciples would be found in the utterly intolerable position of having to treat him as God even though he was not. If they gave him up, then they would lose the power to worship God properly at all (Philippians 3:3).

The Spirit in the Trinity

It is true that the Spirit does the same things, with the same attributes and authority, as God the Father and God the Son; but his share in what happens is distinctly his own. For instance, though he speaks what God speaks, the initiative is not his; it is the Father's (John 14:26; 15:26). Again, as we have seen, whatever he does in making God real to man, it is not his own person that is the focus of attention, it is the Son's. He speaks about the Son, who is not now physically present with us. This is God speaking 'in the third person', speaking *about* the Father and the Son, as he does in fact throughout Scripture. *What* he says when he speaks is not his, it is the Son's. Yet neither the Father nor the Son act or speak without him. He is so essentially God that Jesus said to the Samaritan woman, 'God is Spirit' (John 4:24).

This is obviously nearing the fringe of our powers of thought, but we might venture a step further. The Spirit is God in experience. This experience in our inner life becomes our life as Christians. Now Paul in 1 Corinthians 2:10–11 says,

> The Spirit searches everything, even the depths of God. For what person knows a man's thoughts except the spirit of the man which is in him?

Paul seems to be arguing something like this. In a human being, the only possible experience of the intimate depths of his inner life must go on in his own essential personality, that which alone makes him what he is as a person. This is his 'spirit'. So also God's 'spirit' alone knows the intimate depths of God's inner life, acting like a searchlight on every corner of it. The implication is that the Spirit is to God what a man's spirit is to him – his essential personality: that which makes him what he is as God. The analogy actually goes further. For a man may 'commune with his own heart'. This is apparently possible because he is made in God's image; it is a reflection of a sort of dialogue that goes on in the being of God. The Spirit 'prays to the Father'. The reasoning of the passage in which this idea is found in Scripture (Romans 8:26–27) is even more astonishing: there are at least some occasions when this is actually going on within the groaning hearts of weak believers!

If this can be true of frail believers, it will be infinitely more true of him who came among us and lived as the Son before his Father by the Spirit. The Spirit is the Spirit of Christ as well as the Spirit of the Father. So it seems that it is by the Spirit that the Father and the Son are one in the Godhead. This is what past theologians meant by calling the Spirit the 'vincula amoris', the 'bond of love' which makes the Trinity also One.

This relationship of the Spirit within the Trinity has its effect on the way we receive him as human beings. He is not amongst us as God's Son came amongst us. Jesus is God's Son, and he has a relationship to God which is a kind of pattern for the relationship of all sons to their fathers (see Ephesians 3:14–15, where 'family' is literally 'fatherhood'). Jesus came to this world from the Father. It was an act of obedient self-humbling (Philippians 2:6–8). His saving work was done quite independently of us, while we were still sinners. It was done once for all upon the cross (Hebrews 9:26). On that basis, the Spirit comes to us in response to the request of the ascended Lord Jesus to the Father (John 14:16). So he comes to us from the Father. But in Acts 2:32–33 Peter on the day of Pentecost says this:

> Jesus ... having received from the Father the promise of the Holy Spirit, has poured out this which you see and hear.

So the Spirit comes to us from the Father and the Son, as a result of the love-transactions that go on between them.

The relationship of the Spirit to the Father is therefore different from that of the Son. He is not 'begotten'. In John 15:26, the Spirit is said to 'proceed' from the Father. This is more like the sort of authority or presence that we mean when we sometimes say that 'personality oozes from' a person, or when, as we sometimes remark, 'so-and-so made his presence felt'. There is something of an analogy here in the way any human personality works. There is the person as he is in himself, conducting his life by the values and decisions of his inner life. This could be like God the Father. There is the physical expression of this in our bodily behaviour, our 'thought made flesh' as it were, channelled through time and space. This could be like God the Son. There is also our impact on people, the way people feel our presence, what we mean when we say of someone 'they've got personality'. There are people whose presence gets us all of a dither, however kindly they may behave. Others seem to give us confidence, even though they may act quite strictly with us. This could be likened to the Holy Spirit.

The whole subject of the Trinity is of course a very profound and complex one. Sometimes the discussion seems to become very remote from everyday life. We may be tempted to dismiss it then as useless. At times we may be right. Certainly unless we are called and trained for the job, there is no point in our trying to do the job of the scholar. But we still have to serve God with all the powers of thought we have. There are often matters of truth which appear rather like the Gibeonites did to Joshua in Joshua 9:3–6 – visitors from afar. Joshua treated them fairly casually, and then, too late, discovered they were practically living on his doorstep! Our children now have electronic calculators. Only a few years ago the theory behind the making of these things very abstruse indeed. Good thinking often gets unexpected rewards from the Spirit of truth. On the other hand bad thinking may produce unexpected evils. Slight divergences in doctrine may not do us much harm; but if they are perpetuated among Christians without being checked and examined, they can start causing real trouble.

The Spirit at the End

We shall not always experience God by the Spirit as we do now. The Spirit's work in us is always pressing forward towards a great climax. In Romans 8:23 we are said to have only 'the first fruits of the Spirit' – the beginning of the harvest. God's Spirit clinches the matter when we trust Christ, making us certain of Jesus, but this is only that 'first instalment', the guarantee of something to come (2 Corinthians 1:22). The Spirit creates in us an attitude of expectancy that one day God's righteousness will have its final triumph (Galatians 5:5). He preserves us, so that we may progress, and strive, and grow. The Spirit's 'groaning' within us is part of our experience of longing for that day when our status as God's children will be made public, like the way in the ancient world people would take a child into the market place and declare to all and sundry that this child was now one of their family.

When that day comes, the whole universe will be transformed. At present we do not *see* God's kingdom fully at work. That will come when we see Jesus Christ at his return. The faith which is in us by the Spirit is a loyalty that often seems to have to go against the evidence of our senses (Romans 8:18–25). Our present walk by faith is 'not by sight' (2 Corinthians 5:7) and when, by faith, we look into the future, that faith takes the form of hope. But Paul, as he thinks of the future glory, relegates both faith and hope to the background (1 Corinthians 13:13). So what will be left?

Well, there is one thing that is bound up with faith that is both the fruit of it and the power of it (Galatians 5:22; 5:6). That is love. When we have become truly bound in faith to him who died for us, then, says Paul (Romans 5:5):

> the love of God has been poured into our hearts through the Holy Spirit which has been given to us.

This is a special kind of love. It is not mere attraction, or sentiment, or affection, or passion, or benevolence. It comes from Calvary (1 John 4:10):

> In this is love, not that we loved God, but that he loved us, and sent his son to be the propitiation for our sins.

In us it takes a special form – gratitude. We only love truly in response to his grace. We love, only because he first loved us. Right through the Old Testament the motive for serving God was always to begin with gratitude (1 Chronicles 16:4; Psalm 100:4; etc.). The New Testament takes up the theme. Jesus shows how love comes in gratitude for forgiveness when a 'bad' character showed her love for him in the house of Simon the Pharisee (Luke 7:47–48). The world is condemned for unthankfulness (Romans 1:21). The Christian life is to be punctuated with thanksgiving (Philippians 4:6; Colossians 2:7; etc.). Even as Christians we do not just love from our own natural bent. The love so famously described in 1 Corinthians 13 is spoken of as the highest of gifts (12:31 – 13:1). It is the fruit and gift of the Spirit, the 'love of the Spirit' (Romans 15:30). It comes from the faith which receives mercy at the cross. If this is neglected, or fades, then faith becomes ineffective and idle. 'Faith works by love,' (Galatians 5:6); Christian effort is, in a special way, a 'labour of love' (1 Thessalonians 1:3).

When the Spirit's work of faith and hope in us is finished, we shall still live by the Spirit of grateful love, standing before the throne and before the Lamb, with the song filling our hearts (Revelation 7:12):

Amen! Blessing and glory and wisdom and thanksgiving ... to our God for ever and ever! Amen!

APPENDIX I

Fullness, filling of, or being filled with, the Holy Spirit

In Ephesians 5:18 Paul indicates the condition of a believer in whom the Spirit of the Lord has complete freedom to work, through consecration and faith.

The phrase is used to mean (a) a general tenor of life (so Stephen, Acts 6:3, was 'full'), or (b) a special 'onrush' of the Holy Spirit for some specific situation (so Peter, Acts 4:8, was 'filled'; and perhaps Stephen in 7:55).

Baptism in, or of, the Holy Spirit

Mark 1:8 and parallels refers to the full range of the Holy Spirit's work as it is potentially available at conversion, initiating a person into a life 'in the Spirit', that is, fully surrendered to Christ as Lord, and relying on the effects of the cross through a life of faith for daily experience.

(a) The gospel norm for this is that it should take place fully at conversion (Acts 2:38).

(b) In practice there is often an extended period after conversion in which life is lived largely 'in the flesh' rather than 'in the Spirit'. This may terminate by the believer being introduced into a way of life 'in the Spirit'. (See Romans 7:14 – 8:11; and Galatians 3:2–5; 1 Corinthians 3:1–4.) This may take the form of a definite crisis, which is often called 'the baptism of the Holy Spirit'.

'psycho-physical' or 'charismatic' phenomena
19, the term is also used of an experience of
ment to God, usually with Christian service
view, and associated with glossolalia (i.e.
tongues'). The emphasis is usually on endue-
wer.

e Spirit

2:13 must refer to conversion viewed as the
beginning of the believer's fellowship in the Spirit with other
Christians in the body of Christ. (This phrase is better avoided
as open to too much confusion with baptism *in* or *of* the Holy
Spirit.)

Anointing of the Spirit

Used of Jesus as equipping him for his ministry as 'Christ'
(Luke 4:18, quoting Isaiah 61:1–2). Expressly used in 2 Corinthians 1:22 of others in the New Testament, but could be implied
in the ordination of Timothy (2 Timothy 1:6), so it could be used
in this sense. Used once of all believers in reference to their
common gift of the Spirit in regeneration (1 John 2:27).

Receiving the Holy Spirit

Has a variety of meanings:
(a) The experience of the Spirit in regeneration (Acts 2:38).
(b) Some subsequent specific experience of the Spirit (Acts
    8:15), perhaps to be used particularly in association with an
    act of consecration and faith.
(c) An experience of faith in God to supply the Holy Spirit
    to meet some spiritual need. (Possibly the Greek aorist
    imperative of John 20:22 may refer to this, though note that
    it may be unique to the needs of the apostolic band. It is
    difficult to use this verse dogmatically on the subject.)

The Gift of the Spirit

(a) that which is received in the receiving of the Spirit, as above. Here the 'of' means 'that is'.

(b) Special faculties or abilities or powers given by the Spirit (1 Corinthians 12). Here the 'of' means 'given by'. Usually found in phrases like 'a gift' or 'gifts' of the Spirit.

APPENDIX II

A difficulty in this subject has been the tendency in the church
for its charismatic membership to be alienated from its trained
theological one. Theology gives precision to a Christian's
explanation of his experience, so that the understanding of it can
be passed from generation to generation. It also prefers to deal
with general principles, looking for at least a measure of uni-
formity in Christian experience. The freedom of the Spirit has
always given theologians trouble, and there is always a tendency
in theology to iron out or reject irregular phenomena. The result
is that those who could explain such matters best have not been
those who have most experience of them. Charismatics tend to
claim rather uncritically that they know, for instance, what a
'word of knowledge' is: theologians tend to claim, rather loftily I
think, that nobody knows! We can be thankful that the situation
is improving; but this may explain the rather tentative nature of
these comments.

General comment

It looks as if Paul's list has a certain grading; gifts of larger
significance come first, and the less 'substantial' ones later,
though the logic of the order is not a fixed one.

The utterance of wisdom

It seems likely that this is not the same as wisdom that comes by experience, but rather an ability to speak with exceptional wisdom in especially difficult situations. There would be a certain authority about it, and the person so gifted would find himself speaking more wisely than he understood himself capable. An Old Testament example of this might be the case of Solomon, in 1 Kings 3. Note that it did not stop Solomon doing foolish things (1 Kings 11:1–8)!

Word of Knowledge

This is probably to do with an ability to refer to facts which could not have been known by natural means. Christ's treatment of Nathanael and the Samaritan woman seems to demonstrate this gift (John 1:47–49; 4:17–19). This may be more common than we think. Preachers often get an 'intuition' of some special need in a congregation. I remember once feeling that I should quote a certain passage of scripture to a young woman in deep trouble. She looked at me in amazement, for I hardly knew her. 'How did you know that God has always spoken to me through that text at every crisis of my life?' she said.

Faith

Of course, all our faith is the work of the Spirit, but when a word is isolated in this way, we are entitled to expect that it will have a special meaning. If the gifts are to do with abilities beyond our natural capacity, then the gift of faith will be the ability to trust God for things to happen well beyond the limits of what we would normally think possible. It is not a faith which neces- sarily works miracles itself, but it can trust God that miracles will happen, and act accordingly. Jeremiah's purchase of a field overrun by Babylonian armies might be an example. A modern example is in the growth of George Muller's orphanage.

Gifts of healing

Note the plural, 'gifts'; this is emphasized in 1 Corinthians 12:28

– 'healings'. Obviously there are many different kinds. Some are given to individuals; some are exercised by touch, some by prayer, some by anointing with oil. Others are granted to a group. (E.g. Acts 14:9–10; 19:12; Mark 16:18; Matthew 18:19; James 5:14–15, etc.) Distinguish this from 'faith healing'. Faith has its own power to heal; and this works in most religions from Lourdes to Benares. Distinguish too from spirit-healing. There have been cases of healing in 'spiritist' meetings. There does also seem to be a natural gift of healing, rather like 'green fingers'. The gift of the Spirit is distinctively the power to heal miraculously *in the name of Jesus*. A sick Christian seeking health will always have regard to the question, 'Who is going to get the credit for this?'

Gift of miracle-working

This rather obvious-looking one is not as easy as it seems. For one thing, most miracles are covered by the previous two. The phrase literally means something like 'effecting works of power'. New Testament examples would be Christ's stilling of the storm (Mark 4:39), and the blinding of Elymas (Acts 13:11). The stress is certainly on giving a sample of God's omnipotence.

Gift of prophecy

Paul rates this as the best of the gifts of utterance, if not of all (1 Corinthians 14:1). It is the only gift which we know to have given rise to a particular office in the church, apparently a foundational one (Ephesians 2:20; 3:5; 4:11). Distinguish between the occasional experience of a miraculous phenomenon, and the gift, which is the ability to use it when required, and the office, which is an official position in the church whereby the church regards the person as able to act for the whole community in the exercise of the gift.

Prophecy is not the same as preaching, though preaching may be prophetic. It is not *necessarily* prediction, though most examples in the New Testament include this. It is not necessarily highly ecstatic, though it may tend to be. It is the proclamation of a divine message directly to a particular congregation. The speaker speaks more than he naturally knows, but he does not lose control of himself; indeed he has to learn when to use the gift (1 Corinthians 14:29–31). The characteristics are those of authority, and a peculiar appositeness to the situation. Women are spoken of as having this gift (Acts 21:9).

Gift of discernment of spirits

This is a gift that is easier to understand in circumstances where 'spiritism' or witchcraft or animism is common. One of the characteristics of evil spirits is the practice of deceit (John 8:44; 2 Thessalonians 2:9; Revelation 20:10). It may be beyond the ordinary capacity of a person to be sure of what is going on in a particular situation, though there are tests which can be made, and it is possible for a Christian who is 'in the clear' with God to exercise Christ's authority. He can thus command any spirit to identify himself truly, by addressing the spirit in the name of Jesus. (In general, this sort of thing should not be done by a person on his own; and if such a ministry becomes necessary, then it is best to learn from someone more experienced. There are so many pitfalls.) But the gift of discernment enables a person to detect intuitively whether a 'spiritual' manifestation or message is from God.

The gift of tongues

This is the most elementary of the gifts. It is sometimes spoken of as the 'initial evidence' of a full endowment (often called baptism – see Appendix I) of the Spirit. The doctrine of the *necessity* for this gift is rather doubtfully based on the assertion that there is no case in the New Testament of being flooded with the Spirit for the first time without it. People who make too much fuss about it do tend sometimes to be rather naïve in their Christian attitudes to life. This partly explains why Paul finds the need to regulate its use. It can be a useful means of grace to an individual Christian in a hostile environment. But it is not *in itself* specially Christian; it is present in other religions too.

The phrase in 1 Corinthians 12:10 does speak of 'various kinds' of tongues. Some, like those in Acts 2, are translatable. Occasional cases of this seem to have been reasonably well attested in later times in the church. Other tongues are not translatable. Paul seems to imply this in 1 Corinthians 14:2–12.

Interpretation of tongues

This is speech of a similar type as 'tongues', but gives the sense (not an exact translation) of what has been said in tongues already. It is a gift which makes it possible for speaking in tongues to develop the whole congregation's spiritual life. Paul insists that tongues should not be used in corporate worship unless there is someone present to interpret (1 Corinthians 14:27–28).

It is evident from 1 Corinthians 12–14 that the use of the gifts is to be within the framework of the Holy Spirit's authority. It is to be subject to Scripture, and it is to be regulated by the life and needs of the church.

APPENDIX III

The meaning of the word

'Revival' is sometimes used, especially in the United States, to mean an evangelistic effort or its success. This seems to date from the teaching of Charles Finney. He was himself involved in an outstanding work of revival and this gave his *Lectures on Revival* enormous influence. Unfortunately the impression was drawn from them that all that was needed for revival was the creation of the right human conditions. This has been fostered by the rather man-centred spirit of the age and culture. Possibly if the conditions as Finney actually described them were sought, then we might well have a revival, but not quite in the way we would be led to expect! As it was, the idea of the conditions required degenerated into little more than enthusiasm and a gifted preacher.

The characteristics of authentic revival

It always begins within the life of the church; it is a renewal of life where life once was before. God is felt to be present in an inescapable way, revealing himself in a way that had been neglected in the church's life. Thus the Wesleyan awakening had an emphasis on a free offer of pardon to all, as against the hyper-Calvinism of the day, and the experience of a changed heart, as against the formal religion of the established church. The Welsh revival of 1904 was strongly emotional with singing as its predominating characteristic. This was in stark contrast to the dry theologies that had stifled any spontaneous expression of faith. On the other hand, many of the awakenings of the seventeenth century were closely associated with the preaching of the word and the gospel of the cross. The holiness and love of God are always overwhelmingly present.

The experience of God's grace is unusually infectious, and commonly has what might now be called a 'charismatic' quality about it (I do not mean necessarily anything connected with speaking in tongues) – an unmistakable supernatural quality about it. Witness to the gospel takes on unusual power, far beyond the normal effectiveness of persuasion and proclamation. It reaches out effectively to the surrounding community, so that the most unlikely people are brought to profound repentance and faith.

There is a consequent change in the whole community. England changed its manners radically during the eighteenth century in a way which made it virtually 'odd man out' in Europe for over a century. In the Welsh movement, whole villages went 'dry' where previously in some cases there had been two or three drinking houses in every street.

There is a consequent reaction of hatred and opposition – sometimes (though not always) from obvious vested interests. And there tend to appear rival movements and imitations which can easily cloud the real issues. Revivals do not make a heaven on earth, indeed they tend to show up Christian folly and self-centredness very painfully.

Hindrances to revival

There is undoubtedly a divine sovereignty in revival that makes it difficult to understand why it seems to be arbitrary in its scope and duration. In general one can say that it will stop whenever people begin to think they can patronize it or organize it.

There is evidence that division in a church is a real barrier; but a barrier which the Spirit sometimes overcomes, almost forcibly. Certainly he has no freedom in a feuding church. Doctrine or church organization in themselves are apparently not significant factors, unless they express an attitude in which the Spirit's sovereign grace in Christ is automatically rejected.

Revival is a real possibility in any church that is prepared to allow the Spirit to have his way. But there has to be determined prayer (Luke 11:1–13; Acts 1:14). It has to come from an open heart where confession of sin, and reconciliation with others in forgiveness, are made as required by God (1 John 1:8–9). And there must be a presentation of the gospel, that Christ died for our sins according to the scriptures, that he might be Lord (1 Corinthians 15:1–3; Romans 14:9). In practice what happens is that a point comes when the character of a group's prayer, fellowship and witness takes on a new dimension of power in which they receive an inner drive, vision, longing, burden, which presses them into a revival situation.

In retrospect it becomes obvious that even the praying itself was the work of God.

FURTHER READING

The literature on the subject is enormous, and growing. Older books on spiritual experience are invaluable. Older books on charismatic issues are generally unsatisfactory. Even now, most writings stand fairly definitely on one side or another of a controversy, with a consequent bias. For literature on revival, the best source is the Evangelical Library, London, who can supply guidance for reading.

The list is meant to be introductory. For reading beyond that, Michael Green's *I Believe in the Holy Spirit* (Hodder & Stoughton) is excellent, and has the further bonus of a good classified and annotated booklist.

General

L. Morris, *Spirit of the Living God* (Inter-Varsity Press).

O. Winslow, *The Work of the Holy Spirit* (Banner of Truth). (An early 19th century classic, devotionally and doctrinally rich.)

Stibbs and Packer, *The Spirit within You* (Hodder & Stoughton).

O. Sanders, *The Holy Spirit of Promise* (Marshall, Morgan & Scott).

The Christian Experience of Faith

E. J. Hopkins, *The Law of Liberty in the Spiritual Life* (Marshall, Morgan & Scott).

N. Grubb, *The Law of Faith* (Lutterworth Press).

P. T. Forsyth, *Christian Perfection* (Hodder & Stoughton).

P. Doddridge, *The Rise and Progress of Religion in the Soul* (A heartwarming evangelical classic, recently reprinted.)

E. F. Kevan, *The Saving Work of the Holy Spirit* (Pickering & Inglis).

The church

F. W. Dillistone, *The Holy Spirit in the Life of Today* (Canterbury Press).

J. Goldingay, *The Church and the Gifts of the Spirit* (Grove Books).

D. Watson, *One in the Spirit* (Hodder & Stoughton).

The gifts of the Spirit

L. Christenson, *In the Spirit* (Kingsway Publications).

M. Green, *Cinderella's Betrothal Gifts* (Overseas Missionary Fellowship).

D. Bridge and D. Phypers, *Spiritual Gifts and the Church* (Inter-Varsity Press).

W. Rowe, *One Lord, One Faith* (Puritan Press). This is the fullest statement of a characteristic Pentecostal-type scheme of doctrine I know. One does not need to agree with it all to find interest and benefit.

Revival

Sprague, *Lectures on Revivals of Religion* (Banner of Truth).

J. Burns, *Revivals, their Laws and their Leaders* (Hodder & Stoughton).

J. E. Orr, *The Second Evangelical Awakening* (Marshall, Morgan & Scott).

INDEX